Daily Readings for Lent

Vanessa Herrick

DARTON · LONGMAN + TODD

First published in 2005 by
Darton, Longman and Todd Ltd
1 Spencer Court
140–142 Wandsworth High Street
London
SW18 4JJ

ISBN 0 232 52567 6

A catalogue record for this book is available from the British Library.

Designed by Sandie Boccacci
Phototypeset in 10.25/12.75pt Galliard
Printed and bound in Great Britain by
Page Bros, Norwich, Norfolk

To David
with gratitude and love

Contents

Acknowledgements

I am grateful to a number of people who, in different ways, have supported me in the writing of this book. The idea of a Lent Book for those in ministry emerged as a result of a passing, coffee-time conversation with Virginia Hearn, my editor at DLT, when we were both delegates at a theology conference. I am thankful to her for her encouragement, her editorial wisdom and particularly for her understanding and concern when my mother's illness and death caused a necessary delay to the publishing schedule. Liz Piercy has meticulously seen the book through the latter stages of production, and to her, gratitude is also due.

My colleagues in the Diocese of Ely have been unstinting in their interest and forbearance and I am especially grateful to Bishop Anthony Russell for allowing me to create space within my working schedule for time to write. My secretary, Moira Tuplin, has borne the brunt of my absence from the office: without her presence and efficiency, it would have been impossible to contemplate writing at all. The community of Ridley Hall, Cambridge has been a haven – a place to escape the telephone and know that I would be well looked after.

I am grateful too to the many friends who have prayed for me and prayed for this book in its gestation: to Graham Davies, Ruth Etchells, Eilish Heath, Ivan Mann, Michael and Dorrie Nuttall and Caroline Redman, thank you. Bishop Tim Stevens has been a constant source of strength and I am deeply grateful for his friendship and for his willingness to write the Foreword. He and Dr Bridget Nichols gave some of the material a 'dry run' during Lent this year, and I am indebted to them both for their helpful comments. As always, it is my family – David, Adam and Peter – who have been the most longsuffering: my thankfulness to them, and for them, is beyond measure.

Foreword

Crowds who watch the great open-air dramas of the crucifixion in Leicester city centre each Good Friday tend to be divided into two groups. There are some who are left with the impression of an angry God from whom we are saved by Jesus' death. Others are deeply moved by what they see as a loving God who saves us from ourselves at infinite cost.

It is the latter story of love that Vanessa Herrick invites us to explore in these meditations for each day of Lent. It is a love story illustrated by a great variety of images. We meet familiar figures from the Gospels struggling with their own sense of unloveableness but also friends and colleagues of the author who help us see the living Gospel in our day. All of these figures are on a journey. A journey to the one place where we are confronted with the final revelation of God's love for us – the place of crucifixion and resurrection. The place where ultimately we have to take responsibility for the consequences of discovering our infinite value in the sight of God.

Those of us who are in authorised public ministries need to be reminded of these things. It is for us that Vanessa is primarily writing. As a teacher of theology and a director of ordinands the author knows at first hand how much we need to be constantly reconnected with the source of our life's work. If these sources run dry the demands and claims of a church under pressure can sap and drain the energy and conviction so much needed by those who seek to serve the people of God.

The pressures on the church's public ministry are acute and

intensifying. Much of the contemporary mission discourse encourages the view that given sufficient vision, faithfulness and commitment it will be possible for the church's ministers to grow their congregations. But in these meditations the emphasis is different. For the six weeks of Lent the reader is invited to attend less to the church and more to Jesus as he makes his way to Calvary. In that prayerful, faithful attention we realise once again that we are caught up in the great transforming story of the cross. That our salvation is being worked out for us in all the ordinary events of our lives in which the extraordinary love of God is being made known.

And here lies the only source from which it is possible to minister the word of life. The author's own experience teaches her that praying the Bible daily and attentively recharges and re-equips her for her work. These meditations are an invitation to join her each day of Lent, receiving what the living word has to reveal to us, in our lives. It is through that praying, that receiving of the revelation anew that we may dare to claim to speak the word of life to others.

It is a word often heard in a whisper. In a world where strident religious voices and extremist action appear to sit side by side, we need more than ever the discipline of daily taking up our cross. For in that daily activity of love we begin to hear something different from the strident sounds and to discover at the foot of the cross the truth which does indeed save us from ourselves.

Thou art God: no monarch Thou
Thron'd in easy state to reign;
Thou art God, Whose arms of love
Aching, spent, the world sustain.

THE RT REVD TIM STEVENS
Bishop of Leicester

Introduction

Lent is traditionally a time in the Church's year when Christians take on a particular discipline of reading and prayer. With its roots in the period of preparation undertaken by baptismal candidates in the early Church, and in the period of penitence observed by those who had been excommunicated because of serious sin, the season of Lent quickly became recognised as a helpful time of observance for the whole Christian community as it journeyed, corporately, towards the celebration of Christ's death and resurrection during Holy Week. In worship, it is a season of austerity and restraint; in personal devotion, it is an opportunity to go deeper, to 'give up' time and space and energy to God himself.

This emphasis on a greater discipline in prayer and study has been a positive one, and, in recent years, has produced not only a plethora of devotional and study materials for use by the individual, but also a significant development in the number and range of activities offered by local church communities. Lent Groups, Lent Lunches, Parish Quiet Days and other additional opportunities for corporate prayer such as saying the Midday Office or Compline, have become a normal part of the Lenten cycle in many places. Add to this the increasing desire and impetus to work ecumenically, and Lent has, it seems, become one of the busiest times in the Church's year.

The problem is that all these activities – good as they are in themselves – need to be organised and resourced, and the responsibility for this work tends, rightly, to rest with those who lead and nurture the Christian community in a particular place – be they lay or ordained. The outcome can be that those who hold this responsibility on behalf of others, can find that they have little time or energy really to observe Lent at all. They are so preoccupied with enabling other disciples to keep a good Lent that, for them, it disappears (rather like Christmas) into a fog of extra services and demands that prevent them from really engaging with the season for themselves. And yet *they* are disciples too ...

It is this danger of losing sight of our primary calling to be disciples that is so worrying. We are, first and foremost, invited to be *followers* – not leaders. Of course, the Church needs leaders, just like any other organisation – people to make things happen, to give direction, to speak for the institution or the local community. Yet, sometimes, it seems, the Church is in danger of being seduced by secular models of leadership that fail to recognise the distinctiveness of a priestly calling – be that the personal calling of the ordained, or the corporate calling of the people of God. For a priestly calling demands more than the skills or ability to organise and manage an institution: it demands a willingness to be laid aside for Christ in service of his people and in mission and ministry to his world. Leadership is necessary; but it is only ever *part* of the Christian calling. Ministry, in whatever form it takes, emerges out of *discipleship*; not discipleship out of *ministry*.

If we are disciples first and foremost, then, like Jesus' disciples, we need to walk with him and learn from him. It is, perhaps, to state the obvious, but unless we allow him to feed, nurture and sustain us, except by his grace we shall have nothing to offer to others. *Doing* the things of ministry must be underpinned by the *being* of one who has learnt to sit at Jesus' feet and whose heart has been warmed by his touch. We cannot afford to keep him at a distance.

So it is that this book is written – especially, but by no means exclusively – to encourage those whose calling is primarily to serve others in Christian ministry. This slant is reflected in some of the stories and examples used and in the particular perspectives explored. For those in licensed or authorised ministry, I hope it will 'connect' in a helpful way; for those whose ministry is exercised less 'officially', but no less effectively, I hope it may give insight into some of the pressures ministers may experience, and encourage you to intercede for them. For every disciple of Christ, I trust that this small offering may, by God's Spirit at work in you, lead you further in meditating on God's word and discerning his desire for you each day. More than anything, my aim in offering this book is to encourage and to help build up the people of God as we respond to our corporate vocation to take up our cross and follow Christ.

A note on how to use this book

Most people, I imagine, will have bought this book to use on their own. It might also be used as a focus for reflection at a daily celebration of the Eucharist or read at a Midday Office. Alternatively, it could form the basis for reflection and discussion at a weekly Lent Group or a ministers' meeting. The readings chosen for each day are those from the Daily Eucharistic Lectionary of the Revised Common Lectionary. For the most part the readings coincide with those in the Roman Missal, although on occasion a slightly longer passage has been suggested than is printed therein. The Psalms are numbered according to the NRSV version of the Bible. Reflections have been included for Sundays in Years A, B and C. There are two points in the cycle of readings where there is a significant divergence in the readings set for the day. First, the readings for the Second Sunday of Lent in the Roman Calendar focus on the story of the Transfiguration and these have been included in the main text of the book. In the Anglican cycle, the readings set for this particular Sunday are completely different and may be found, with appropriate reflections, in the Appendix. The second point of divergence is on the Tuesday and Wednesday of Holy Week: alternatives here, and other more minor variations, are indicated in the main text of the book.

VANESSA HERRICK
June 2005

THE COLLECT FOR THE THIRD SUNDAY OF LENT

Almighty God,
whose most dear Son went not up to joy
but first he suffered pain,
and entered not into glory before he was crucified:
mercifully grant that we, walking in the way of the cross,
may find it none other than the way of life and peace;
through Jesus Christ your Son our Lord,
who is alive and reigns with you,
in the unity of the Holy Spirit,
one God, now and for ever.
Amen.

ASH WEDNESDAY

Serving the one who sees in secret

Joel 2:1–2, 12–17 or Isaiah 58:1–12
Psalm 51:1–18
2 Corinthians 5:20b – 6:10
Matthew 6:1–6, 16–21

There's something of a dilemma about Ash Wednesday. On the one hand it's one of those days when it seems right to 'focus inward', to reflect, like the Psalmist, on our 'iniquity', 'sin' and 'transgressions', and to acknowledge our complete dependence on the abundant mercy and steadfast love of God. Indeed, the reciting of Psalm 51 in daily prayer throughout the season of Lent acts as a refrain, constantly drawing us back to that place of smallness, weakness and repentance. In our innermost, secret place of the heart, we know our need of God.

On the other hand, it's one of those days in the Church's calendar when we are invited, individually and corporately, to 'bear the sign', to be most 'public', most 'outward' in the exercise of our faith. To receive the sign of the cross in ash on our forehead, or to administer it to others, can be both moving and convicting; to hear or speak the words, 'Dust you are and to dust you shall return: turn away from sin and follow Christ' can be both stark in its directness and challenging in its command. Yet, 'ashing', as it is often called, is a public act of devotion which can seem to run counter to Jesus' insistence that we should not practise our piety before others 'in order to be seen by them'.

Perhaps, as so often, the problem begins to be resolved

when we take the focus off ourselves and concentrate instead on God? Two things emerge from today's readings that speak to this 'inward–outward' dilemma: first, God not only *sees* in secret, but he *is* in secret. Whether or not we are marked with an ashen cross on the *outside*, God knows us from the *inside* – and that's where he chooses to be: he himself, *is* in the secret places of our heart, and nothing can be hidden from him. Second, God is not impressed by mere religiosity – be that individual or corporate. Not only does he see through outward appearances to the hearts of persons and communities, but he also expects piety to be matched by practice. God, and the things of God, become *real* as we serve others.

So, yes, Lent *is* a time for self-examination and reflection, but it is also an opportunity to review in what way and to what extent that private, 'inward-focus' bears fruit in the public 'outward-focus' of service. We can be so intent upon the *outward* demands of the Lenten season that we miss meeting God where he already *is*, in the secret place. On the other hand, those who follow Christ can also run the risk of imbuing the Lenten season with a self-indulgence that closes their eyes to the ongoing necessity of an *active* discipleship. Perhaps 'serving the one who sees in secret' holds the key to that dilemma?

The human heart is the focal point from which history must be transfigured; only the sanctified human being can sanctify the world.[1]

THURSDAY AFTER ASH WEDNESDAY

Choose life

Deuteronomy 30:15–end
Psalm 1
Luke 9:22–25

St Luke's insertion of the little word 'daily' after Jesus' invitation to his would-be disciples to 'take up their cross' is a helpful injunction on this second day of Lent. Ash Wednesday is one thing: to find yourself 'in the secret place' on day two, and recognise that it's a case of 'me and God' for the next six and a half weeks is quite another! Not that one is *really* alone: the Spirit who makes us one in Christ holds us together by invisible cords even when we don't realise it. Yet, taking up our cross *daily* requires a discipline and a strength that doesn't come naturally. There are many potential distractions and alternatives: the path of wickedness and scoffing, for example, where we pour scorn on the feeble attempts of others and become suffused in our own self-righteousness; or being 'led astray to bow down to other gods and serve them', so closing our hearts and ears to the commands of God. So, we have to choose. And it is in that *choosing*, in that expressed desire – however quavering – to follow Christ each day, that we are met with the abundance of grace and mercy we need.

To choose to take up our cross daily is, paradoxically, to choose life – but only if it consists in taking up our *particular* cross, and only if it is coupled with the dynamic of *following Christ* from day to day. Trying to carry other people's crosses and then standing still with them is not what it's about. Pastoral concern for our fellow-disciples is right and good; but our aim should only ever be to *help* them carry their cross, not to take all of their crosses upon ourselves. We can assist those we care about but we cannot walk the road for them. Even Simon of Cyrene could only help Jesus carry his cross on the road to Golgotha: ultimately, Jesus had to carry it himself.

Those who exercise pastoral ministry know the trap all too well: weighed down by the troubles of friends and parishioners to the extent that we lose sight of our own 'cross' – perhaps even fooling ourselves that we don't have one – we end up with little or no energy to follow Christ at all, let alone *daily*! Immobility sets in. For the truth is that the only one who can carry any of us is Jesus himself – 'Take my yoke upon you and learn from me ...' To try to do anything else leads at best to exhaustion, at worst, into the trap of that very 'scoffing' and self-righteousness we so want to avoid. To 'choose life' is to recognise our responsibility *daily* to carry our *own* cross, not to shy away from it or to indulge in it; but to invite the one who carried *his* own to sustain us and travel with us on the way.

There is but one road to the kingdom of God – a cross, voluntary or involuntary.[2]

FRIDAY AFTER ASH WEDNESDAY

Right religion is not enough

Isaiah 58:1–9
Psalm 51:1–5, 17–18
Matthew 9:14–15

Some years ago, a lively charismatic congregation received a word of prophecy encouraging them to turn a large, Victorian rectory into a church and community centre, so giving them facilities with which to extend their practical work and Christian witness among the people of their parish and town. God was calling his people into action and equipping them for the task of 'loosing the bonds of injustice', 'letting the oppressed go free', 'sharing bread with the hungry' and 'bringing the homeless poor into their own house'. They were exciting times.

Not many miles away, another congregation had reached a stalemate in a protracted debate about the effects of introducing a modern-language liturgy into the established and widely appreciated musical tradition of their parish. There were those who saw the need to make the language of services more accessible; there were others for whom any deviation from the words of the *Book of Common Prayer* would be an act of both liturgical and musical sacrilege. They were bogged down in their own religious world, delighting – in their own way – to draw near to God, but feeling ignored and unnoticed by him. What had gone wrong?

According to Isaiah, the people of Judah had reached a similar state: right religion was getting in the way of righteousness. Self-interest, albeit for laudable religious reasons, was getting in the way of the true calling of the people of God. What was needed was someone prepared to speak out and say that God looks for evidence of right *action* as well as right *religion*. The inward- and outward-focus needed to be held in balance: right religion on its own was not enough.

Having the courage to *be* that voice is not easy. Prophets are rarely welcomed, whether in their own town or not! Yet, Christian history has shown time and again that when right religion gets in the way of right action, the Church has lost its way and God looks on in judgement. Sometimes it will be the leader of a community who speaks out, who is prepared to proclaim to God's people the need to 'rebuild the walls of Jerusalem' as well as offer a 'broken and contrite heart'. Sometimes it will be members of the community who, courageously, bring a community back to the joyful heart of the faith and remind them what they are there for. Jesus had little time for right religion: he rebuffed the critical disciples of John who came complaining about his own disciples' apparent lack of solemnity and piety. Instead, he encouraged their joy and excitement in doing his work in the world. Perhaps, sometimes, we need to pray for courage to do the same?

God does not give his joy to us for ourselves alone, and if we could possess himself for ourselves alone, we would not possess him at all. Any joy that does not overflow from our souls and help other people to rejoice in God does not come to us from God.[3]

SATURDAY AFTER ASH WEDNESDAY

I am devoted to you

Isaiah 58:9b–end
Psalm 86:1–7
Luke 5:27–32

Devotion is not a word we hear very often. It suggests a long-term, intense and profound dedication to someone or something that is, so often, hidden, taken for granted, unnoticed. When we witness it – for example, in the faithful care of an ageing parent or a handicapped child – we are not only impressed, and even convicted of our own casual shallowness, but made aware again of the superficiality and fleetingness of much that constitutes our contemporary culture. It can seem as if 'Here today and gone tomorrow' applies as much to our relationships and commitments as it does to the latest technological or scientific advance.

Yet devotion is very much a part of the calling of those who are disciples of the living God; and devotion breeds joy. The Psalmist cries out to Yahweh, pouring out his anxiety in the face of trouble and his trust in God's goodness, mercy and love. Through his prophet, God urges his people to a fervent service of the poor and the oppressed, and draws them away from self-interest and gain to a renewed honouring of the Sabbath. In the call of Matthew, we witness the new birth of a life's journey consecrated to following Jesus Christ and preaching the kingdom; and the sign of that new beginning is a joyful celebration with the outcasts and sinners – those with whom Matthew could so easily identify because, until that moment, he had been one of them.

We are shy of devotion. We think we will be thought odd, old-fashioned, peculiar. Yet, devotion is a gift. The desire even to take time each day to reflect on these readings is, first, God's gift to you. You did not make it happen; *he* did. For devotion is rooted in, and the fruit of, a covenant relationship with him. It is not something we can 'rustle up' out of our own resources – making ourselves more holy. No, *he* is the initiator; and it is only because *he is devoted to us* that we can in any way respond to him and know his joy in our hearts.

Perhaps it is time to ponder this close connection between devotion and joy? Perhaps it is because we are so inhibited, even diffident, about appearing to be 'too committed' that we not only fail to perceive God's priorities, but also miss out on that deep, inner joy that can sustain us through the pressures and demands of daily living? Jesus knew that joy in his relationship with his heavenly Father. He was devoted to the Father's will, obedient to his call and utterly committed to walking in the way of the cross, with all that that would mean for him. The one who calls us knows what devotion means. Jesus' invitation to Matthew was simple and direct: 'Follow me', he said. And he did. You can't get more devoted than that.

Joy is the serious business of heaven.[4]

FIRST WEEK OF LENT

Take up thy cross, the Saviour said,
If thou wouldst my disciple be;
Deny thyself, the world forsake,
And humbly follow after me.

FIRST SUNDAY OF LENT (YEAR A)

You are a hiding place for me

Genesis 2:15–17; 3:1–7
Psalm 32 (or Psalm 51)
Romans 5:12–19
Matthew 4:1–11

He had never imagined it could happen to him ... a man of the cloth, an upright citizen, a pillar of the community. Yet here he was, charged with embezzling church funds, stripped of his job and his dignity, facing imprisonment and covered in shame. Sam had been in post for seven years. Seven years; seven churches to look after; seven church councils to oversee; seven sets of accounts to entice him as he tried to satisfy his need for excitement and purpose by escaping into the thrill of gambling and alcohol. He was exhausted, disheartened, disillusioned. He longed for rest; he was desperate for affirmation and encouragement as he tried, hopelessly, to recover some sense of direction and meaning in his life. And he was tired of hiding. At least, now, they all knew ...

The perceived need to hide is a strong theme in today's readings. It follows swiftly on from Adam and Eve's disobedience in the Garden of Eden; Eve is lured by the desire for knowledge and gives in, taking Adam and the whole human race with her. The Psalmist (Psalm 32) tries to hide his sin until he discovers, through confession and repentance, that God himself becomes a 'hiding place' for him, a place of forgiveness, security and steadfast love. In the meantime, however, temptations continue, deception persists and exhausted human frailty succumbs again.

Yet in Matthew's account of Jesus' temptations in the wilderness, we discover an alternative possibility. For we realise (as did the people of Israel on their long trek to the promised land), that the wilderness, and the temptations it so often embodies, is not only a place of testing and difficulty, but can become a place of growth and maturity in the ways of God. Rather than a place of despair and misery, the wilderness becomes a locus of hope and anticipation as, in Christ, and through the power of God's Spirit speaking through the written and the living word, evil is overcome, truth is upheld and God's ministering angels bring relief and comfort to his chosen. Jesus was no different from us: he was tempted to satisfy his bodily desires, to test whether God would *really* keep his promises, and to wield power and influence over those around him. In the 'apple of Eden' each of these temptations is implicit, and it is an 'apple' we each long to taste from time to time.

Perhaps Sam's story is more extreme than most, but it illustrates something of the pressure, the loneliness, the temptations and the sheer slog of ministry in today's world. In some ways, it is a story shared by many Christian people, faithful followers of Jesus Christ, who have lost their way (as the Anglican ordination liturgy puts it) 'in the wilderness of this world's temptations and ... confusions'. We may want to hide. We may fear being exposed. Before God, we are already. We do well to remember that our true 'hiding place' longs to preserve us from trouble and surround us with cries of deliverance.

From the moment Christ went out into the desert to be tempted, the loneliness, the temptation and the hunger of every man and woman became the loneliness, the temptation and hunger of Christ.[5]

FIRST SUNDAY OF LENT (YEAR B)

Stop and stare

Genesis 9:8–17
Psalm 25:1–10
1 Peter 3:18–22
Mark 1:9–15

It was one of those moments when you simply had to rush outside and wait and stop and stare. There, arced over the golden, stone tower of Ely Cathedral was a double-rainbow – a glorious finale to a summer storm that had left the garden soaked and the roads and pathways steaming. There's something very special about a rainbow. It's not just its physical beauty – the diffraction of light that creates such a wonderful spectrum from red to deep blue. It's not just that it is so often set against a dark grey sky, deepening the intensity of the colours in contrast to the brightness of the sun, now streaming across the sodden landscape. It's that a rainbow says something about God. It says, he is still interested; he still cares about his creation; he has not forgotten us; and he longs for us to come back to him.

Today's readings speak to us of a God who waits, a God who saves, and a God who proclaims good news. The people of the earth had turned their backs on God. He waited and waited for them to repent, but they would not. Only Noah was righteous: only Noah and his close family would be saved. Yet, in his Covenant with Noah, God promises never again to destroy the earth by a flood – and the rainbow is there to remind both him and the creation of his promise. St Peter also tells his readers of God's endless patience and mercy, for 'in the spirit' Christ went to proclaim salvation even to those spirits who had refused to believe. In our Gospel reading, Jesus' message is clear and insistent: 'The time is fulfilled, and the kingdom of God has come near; repent, and believe in the good news.' However reluctant his hearers, God doesn't give up on them, but goes out of his way to draw them back into right relationship with him.

Paradoxically, an active Christian ministry can be precisely the means by which we are prevented from coming back to God. There is too much to do, too much to prepare. The Church needs us – to lead groups, to organise hunger lunches, to prepare for the liturgy, to give a talk, to rehearse special music, to support our ecumenical friends – and so on. We don't have time. We cannot pray. So we don't *really* have to face ourselves and see ourselves as God sees us. We're doing everything for him – or so we think – but we won't let him do anything for us. We have turned our backs, and buried ourselves in activity.

Perhaps the rainbow reminds us that God has *not* forgotten. He is still interested; he still cares; and he longs for us to come back to him. Perhaps God wants us, sometimes, just to wait and stop and stare?

I have often said to you, and I now say once more: Renounce yourself, surrender yourself, and you shall enjoy great inner peace. Give all for all, look for nothing, ask nothing in return: rest purely and trustingly in Me, and you shall possess Me.[6]

FIRST SUNDAY OF LENT (YEAR C)

On the margins

Deuteronomy 26:1–11
Psalm 91:1–2, 9–16
Romans 10:8b–13
Luke 4:1–13

There's a church in Boston, Massachusetts, which is a little bit different to most. It doesn't meet in a building: it meets in the park. They don't use books or overhead projectors: most of them can't read. The people who come don't wear their 'Sunday best': they don't *have* 'Sunday best'. Yet the worship is lively, the preaching is good and the congregation comes, week after week, because they know that they matter and that God cares about them. They are addicts, drunkards, homeless, prostitutes, unemployed and ex-cons; but the woman priest and the Christian community that shares in welcoming them has been called to minister on the margins of society, and their ministry is bearing abundant fruit. Every Sunday, some two hundred people gather in the park, come rain or shine, to talk about the things of God and give thanks for his blessings and love.

The people of Israel knew what it was to be on the margins. A nomadic people, they found themselves as a minority in Egypt, aliens under an oppressive regime and treated harshly as slaves. They cried out to God and he saved them, bringing them – after many years of wilderness wanderings – to settle in their promised land. God protected and blessed them and now called them to offer thanksgiving to him by giving him the first-fruits of the harvest. Not only that: they, once aliens themselves, are to celebrate all the bounty that the Lord has given and share it with the aliens who now reside in *their* land. They are to show that the God who had protected them from harm, cares about those who are now on the margins of *their* society. For all people who call on God's name will be saved (as St Paul later reminds us), and the barriers we might put up of class, creed, appearance or ethnic origin mean absolutely *nothing* to him.

On this first Sunday in Lent, it is worth remembering that when the Spirit led Jesus out into the wilderness, immediately after his baptism, he was leading him out onto the margins. It is *there* that his ministry really began. It began with prayer and contemplation; with fasting and pondering; with the agony of hunger and thirst and the ecstasy of communion with his heavenly Father; with the defeat of Satan and the affirmation of his calling as Son of Man and Son of God. Ministry for those who follow in his footsteps will be just as demanding. For God shows no partiality. The aliens and strangers of our own day need to know God's love and salvation just as much as we do – the immigrants, the asylum seekers, the poor – as well as the misfits of our towns and cities. Like the Church in the Park in Boston, like the stranger in the promised land, like Jew and Greek, like Jesus in the wilderness – it is there, on the margins, that our ministry *really* begins.

You cannot claim to worship Jesus in the tabernacle if you do not pity Jesus in the slum …[7]

MONDAY IN WEEK 1

True lovers?

Leviticus 19:1–2, 11–18
Psalm 19:7–end
Matthew 25:31–end

It is only rarely that St Valentine's Day falls within Lent. Yet in the secular world, it is probably the most significant date between Christmas and Easter. The appearance of the first display of red hearts and kisses on newsagents' and supermarket shelves, long before the sale-price Christmas cards have disappeared, confirms that this day for 'lovers' has become firmly established in the retail strategies of the commercial world. 'Love' makes money.

But there is a significant difference between the way most people think of 'love' and today's readings. The majority of those who send or receive cards or flowers or chocolates on the Feast of St Valentine, think of 'love' in terms of personal, individual feelings and commitments. The message, both in Leviticus and on the lips of Jesus, is that 'love' is to be characteristic of a *community's* way of life as well. 'You shall be holy' and 'You shall love your neighbour as yourself' are words addressed to 'all the congregation of the people of Israel'. Moreover, the image of Christ's judgement of the sheep and the goats is applied to the gathering of the *nations* before him – *not* individual people.

The personal dimension of love is crucial: loving another, and knowing that you are loved, is part of what makes us human. Yet there is so much more to be said. When Jesus encourages his disciples to see *him* in the hungry, the stranger, the sick and the prisoner, he opens up the possibility of a personal love that not only identifies Christ with all who suffer, but that transcends individualism and allows *communities* to become 'lovers' too. The personal and the corporate must be held together: without the first, love becomes mere philanthropy; without the second, we collude with a world-view that runs counter to God's call to his people.

Many churches have focused their work as 'lovers' in pastoral and social care in their localities, through support of the very young, the homeless and the elderly. Perhaps we are less good at recognising our need to become 'lovers' in the realm of national and international affairs, prepared to challenge the structures and strictures of a world where the question of whether 'love makes money' may lurk, silently, behind the activities of political and commercial bodies alike. For as long as we, corporately, fail to love our neighbour as ourselves, we sit under God's judgement and risk his eternal punishment. For as long as we fail to see Christ in them, we inoculate ourselves against the pain of sharing in their sufferings and his. Ministers in the Church of God hold a particular responsibility both to encourage and to enable disciples to become true lovers – at every level of society – and not just in the way card manufacturers would like us to be.

The Indentured Coolie

There he crouched
Back and arms scarred, like a hunted thing,
Terror-stricken.
All within me surged towards him
While the tears rushed.
Then, a change.
Through his eyes I saw Thy glorious face –
Ah, the wonder!
Calm, unveiled in deathless beauty,
Lord of sorrow.[8]

TUESDAY IN WEEK 1

Word processing?

Isaiah 55:10–11
Psalm 34:4–6, 21–22
Matthew 6:7–15

It has been estimated that by the age of two, a child has heard and begun to learn the use of some 150 to 300 different words. By the age of five, that has increased to 2,000 and by sixteen, it has reached between 12,000 and 15,000. Each day, through our letter boxes and the media, we are bombarded with yet more words (and images) designed to stimulate our brains into thinking, assessing, criticising and (more often than not) *desiring*, any number of products, packages, persons or policies. In the Church we produce reports, liturgies, press releases and (dare I say it) books, until there seems little more to be said; and we are trained to generate yet more words in notices, church magazines, letters and sermons. We have become masters and mistresses of word processing, in bondage to our computers, tied to the necessities of language – to write and to print and to speak, in the hope that something, somewhere, somehow will 'get through'. Yet, we run the risk that our words drown out the message and our prose obscures the point. Our words have become a 'procession' that seems to know neither its origin nor its goal.

The prophet Isaiah tells a different story. When *God* speaks, every syllable is loaded; nothing is wasted; all is effective. His word to his people is both powerful and fruitful and needs to be taken seriously. There is no 'emptiness', no lack of purpose here; God's word 'shall accomplish that which I purpose, and succeed in the thing for which I sent it.' As Jesus himself knew, every word that proceeds from the mouth of *God* knows where it has come from and knows where it is going. What a contrast to the 'empty phrases' of the prayers of the Gentiles, about which he speaks to his disciples! Here are words which fall over themselves as they are spewed out in the vain hope that their sheer abundance will sway the mind and will of God. Yet *theirs* is a 'procession' that has lost its way ...

We do well to ponder our use of words. First, when we 'speak out' the word of God to others, whether in written or spoken form, whether in teaching or in pastoral care, do we *expect* it to be effective and fruitful? Second, are we sometimes as guilty as the 'Gentiles' of 'heaping up empty phrases', thinking we will be heard because of our many words? Have we lost the Psalmist's sense of trust in the deliverance of God? Or are we caught up in a frenzy of 'word processing' – actual and metaphorical – that prevents us from really communicating with the God who knows what we need before we ask him?

Jesus warns us about 'babbling on' in our prayers as if the more we pray, the more likely we are to be heard ... It is not the quantity, but the reality that matters.[9]

WEDNESDAY IN WEEK 1

Sign language

Jonah 3
Psalm 51:1–5, 17–18
Luke 11:29–32

If we need to be careful about our use of words, perhaps we should consider signs instead? We are surrounded by them – and by so many that, sometimes, we don't even notice they are there. If you travel to work by car, or walk the same streets each day to get to work or school or a friend's house, you don't examine every traffic sign or nameplate to check that you're going in the right direction. You know the route. Similarly, if you see the same advertising hoarding or shop-front as you pass by each day, or hear the same jingle on the radio whenever you switch it on, you blank out the message and become immune to its significance. You've seen it or heard it all before. If you are driving in a strange town or visiting someone whose house you've never been to, however, you take care to check that you've not missed a turning. You look for the signs – some reassurance that you're still heading in the right direction.

Sometimes, however, the signs can stare us in the face and we *still* don't see them – particularly if they appear in unexpected ways or places. The increasingly large crowd who followed Jesus around the country wanted to be sure that Messiah had come; but they were not convinced. They hadn't seen the right sort of signs: no political campaigning; no gathering of zealous radicals; no evidence to suggest that Jesus was about to overthrow the regime. Instead, a strange

Galilean carpenter who spoke of a Kingdom of Heaven and of himself as the Son of Man. The sign language was all wrong.

In today's readings, signs come not in the form of billboards or advertising slogans, but in the form of *people*. Jonah was a sign of the impending judgement of God; first to the terrified sailors on the boat sailing from Joppa to Tarshish (even as he ran away, he was a sign for God!); and then as he risked walking into the heart of the great city of Nineveh, declaring God's anger and punishment. The King of Nineveh was a sign for his people, rising from his throne, removing his robe, declaring a solemn fast and covering himself in sackcloth and ashes – leading them by example in his response to the call to repentance. The Son of Man – something far greater than Solomon and Jonah – became a sign for his own generation, and all generations to come, of the judgement and mercy of God. He stared them in the face; he spoke the words of his Father; and *still* they could not see or hear. The sign language was all wrong.

In a culture where we are inundated with messages and signs to the extent that we train ourselves not to notice them, it is worth remembering that *people* – *who* they are and *how* they are – can often speak louder than any words or actions. They speak a sign language all of their own. And that's true for ministers and disciples alike.

It is our being, as well as our doing, that is at the heart of our priestly identity and character.[10]

THURSDAY IN WEEK 1

Getting involved with God

Esther 14:1–5, 12–14 (or Isaiah 55:6–9)
Psalm 138
Matthew 7:7–12

The reluctance of witnesses to come forward to give evidence in court is but one indication of a society that prefers not to 'get involved'. It's as if keeping a distance is safer, healthier even, and means that we can get on with our private lives without too many hassles. The counsel given to those in the caring professions carries a similar underlying message: 'Preserve yourself, or you will be sucked into the affairs of others in a way you will not be able to bear.' It is sound advice in some ways; but it masks a pervasive trend towards individualism and away from taking responsibility for the happiness and welfare of our fellow human beings. 'Getting involved' is best avoided – or so people would have us think.

But what about getting involved with God? Today's readings encourage a different attitude. Isaiah's command and Matthew's urging suggest an almost irresistible imperative to seek God: 'Seek the Lord ... call upon him ...'; 'Ask ... search ... knock ...' The Psalmist exclaims: 'I give you thanks, O Lord, with my whole heart' – a wholeheartedness that will involve our lips, our eyes and our hands – our words, our attitudes and our actions – not just some distant, abstract acknowledgement of who God is and what he has done.

One of the ways in which Christians through the ages have demonstrated their desire to 'get involved with God' is through the prayer of contemplation. It demands a commitment of time, purpose and presence that speaks eloquently, in our own age, of a desire to resist the temptation to keep a distance from God. For God has no wish to keep his distance from us. He answers our call, regards the lowly, and stretches out his hand towards those in trouble. His steadfast love endures forever, he pardons the sinner and gives good things to those who ask him. He chose to 'get involved' with us in the person of Jesus Christ. His ways are *not* our ways, and for that we can be thankful.

The prayer of contemplation does not come easily. It is, itself, a gift from God and like all God's gifts, it must be received before it can be offered back with delight and joy. For many, a first step will simply be to express a desire to draw closer to God: we may meditate on a phrase of Scripture; we may focus on an image or symbol; we may contemplate an icon of Christ; we may do all or none of these things. What matters is that we do not allow *our ways* to get in the way of *God's ways.* The world may tell us to keep our distance from him: but God longs for us to 'get involved'.

It is not I who wanted prayer. It is he who wanted it. It is not I who have looked for him. It is he who has looked for me first ... The hope on which my prayer rests is in the fact that it is he who wants it. And if I go to keep the appointment it is because he is already there waiting for me.[11]

FRIDAY IN WEEK 1

Out of the depths

Ezekiel 18:21–28
Psalm 130
Matthew 5:20–26

It seems it is not uncommon for Christian ministers to suffer from depression. Perhaps it is something to do with the sort of people God calls; perhaps it is a reflection of the pressures so many find themselves under from day to day. Either way (and it is probably both), there can sometimes be a serious mismatch between the person people see on the outside and their state of mind and heart and soul on the inside. An Anglican colleague of mine suffered from depression for several months as he struggled to come to terms with who he really was. Yet, for most of that time, he continued to function as a priest – leading worship, preaching, teaching, organising parish events and ministering to the dying and the bereaved. The strain – both for him and his family – was immense.

When the Psalmist writes, 'Out of the depths I cry to you, O Lord,' he exclaims words that many Christian ministers long to be able to echo, and yet their mouths are struck dumb because they dare not let their cry be heard by those around them. For it is a cry that reveals how far short they fall. They are weighed down by an awareness of their own failure and haunted by the possibility of being found out. Their sinfulness is great; they simply don't match up to what is expected of them. They know they risk the judgement of God for their unrighteousness (as Ezekiel makes plain), and they can find it a struggle to keep relationships in good order with those around them. No wonder they long to cry 'out of the depths'.

Yet here is a cry not of despair, but of hope. For its emphasis is on the forgiveness, steadfast love and redeeming power of God, not just for an individual, but for a whole community. It's as if the cry of the Psalmist for *himself* makes it possible for the nation as a whole to cry out from the depths to the God who saves, and to discover that they too can be redeemed. It is a cry that is uttered *on the way to worship* – just at the point where one might expect holiness and joy rather than self-recrimination and anguish – one that recognises that forgiveness leads to *reverence* and waiting on God, and to a true and 'hope-full' understanding of his word. It is a cry that releases others to call out to the one who redeems.

Those who suffer from depression are not necessarily a stumbling block to other people. On the contrary, their willingness to be vulnerable may be the very sign that points others to a loving and saving God.

Lord, I acknowledge the depth of pain;
keep me also able to see
the depth and height
and length and breadth
– the Father's all-embracing love;
and let me then stay with pain and love
until each is transfigured
one into the other
as lovers must.[12]

SATURDAY IN WEEK 1

Be perfect

Deuteronomy 26:16–end
Psalm 119:1–8
Matthew 5:43–end

A close friend of mine has a large black and white poster on his study wall. It is a photograph of a man holding a baby: both are naked, and the child looks up, wide-eyed, focusing intently on the man's face. It is a picture of power and vulnerability; strength and smallness; steadiness and unwavering trust. It is a picture of wonder, amazement and awe as a grown man looks on and sees the perfection of his new-born son. It is a picture of commitment, dependency and of a profound, unspoken love. Parents sometimes describe their new-born infant as 'perfect'; and whatever one's doctrine of original sin, it is hard to question the innocence of such a treasured child, even though (as every parent knows), such innocence can sometimes seem short-lived!

Today's reading from Deuteronomy reminds us of the two-way nature of God's covenant with his people Israel: God commits himself to them *provided that* they walk in his ways and are obedient to his commands. If they *do*, they will be his 'treasured people ... set high above all nations that he had made, in praise and in fame and in honour'. And if they don't ... well, the Old Testament narrative tells its own tale. Commitment demands holiness and obedience in response, and God's people repeatedly fall short. Matthew's Gospel, however, puts a different slant on things. No longer is God's generous love to be limited to his chosen people or to those who keep his commandments. Moreover, in the new order, Jesus' followers are to reflect this generous loving of enemies and persecutors, of the evil and the good, of the righteous and the unrighteous, in a way that completely overturns the expectations of God's 'treasured people': they are to love those who do not love them back, and greet those who ignore them.

Christian ministers are often expected to be perfect. They, their congregations and the wider community, know that they are not. Yet the news media constantly seeks to undermine their effectiveness in ministry by pointing out their faults – great and small – so implying that *nothing* of who they are or what they do is of any worth. It is the old-covenant image of a God-forsaken people who fail because they cannot keep all the rules. To his beleaguered sons and daughters, and to those – within and without the Church – who persecute them, God says afresh: 'You are a treasured people.' For 'being perfect' is not a permanent state: it is a way of holiness, a way of life. We may not succeed in keeping all the rules; we may feel vulnerable, small and dependent. Yet God looks on us and sees a child made perfect in Christ – a perfection that comes to its full fruition as we begin to look on others in the same way.

What is it that the Father has told us through the Son? What is it that the Son has said to us in the Father's name? First of all, He has given us a summons to perfection.[13]

SECOND WEEK OF LENT

Take up thy cross; let not its weight
Fill thy weak spirit with alarm;
His strength shall bear thy spirit up,
And brace thy heart, and nerve thine arm.

SECOND SUNDAY OF LENT (YEAR A)*

It is good to be here

Genesis 12:1–4
Psalm 33:4–5, 18–20, 22
2 Timothy 1:8–10
Matthew 17:1–9

A couple of years ago, my husband and I stayed with friends in South Africa. We had only known them a short while, but they had quickly become very dear to us and we longed to visit them in their own country. The long-anticipated moment finally arrived and we were able to greet them in person again. 'It is good to be here,' I said, as we embraced in greeting. That sense of rightness, of goodness, of fulfilment is one that each of us experiences from time to time. It may be a special holiday in a fascinating place, a gathering of friends or family to celebrate an anniversary, or the opportunity to be present at an historic state occasion: whatever the event, one has a sense of the significance of the moment and it is something to savour.

When Peter exclaimed, on the Mount of Transfiguration, 'Lord, it is good for us to be here!' it was, more than anything, an exclamation of joy. Struck with a sense of wonder and awe, Peter is overwhelmed by the dazzling presence of God and there is only one response – to fall at his feet and worship, as Jesus is transfigured before him. There is joy; but there is also fear, as a cloud overshadows them and a

* For readings for the Second Sunday of Lent according to the Anglican cycle, see Appendix.

heavenly voice is heard. Yet, this fear is not negative; it is about reverence and respect rather than terror or alarm, for in the Jewish understanding, fear is matched by God's grace. Peter, in his weakness, can face this powerful vision of the glory of God, aware that he is accepted and loved.

The trouble is, these moments of encounter with God do not last forever. Or do they? How often do we even come apart and go to the mountain with Jesus, eager and expectant, longing to see his glory? How often in our worship do we have that sense of rightness, of goodness, of fulfilment, when we can genuinely say, 'Lord, it is good for us to be here!'? How often is our participation in, or leading of, worship overshadowed by anxiety about 'getting it right', so that we neither hear God's voice, nor see his glory? Peter's experience on the Mount of Transfiguration reminds us that both in personal prayer and corporate worship, the glory of God may, indeed, be revealed. Perhaps, even more, it reminds us that the glory of God is present in the ordinary matters of daily living. The problem is, we separate worship from the rest of life; we disconnect the extraordinary from the ordinary. What God offers us, this Lent, is the grace to begin to unite the two again, so that we find ourselves saying, many, many times a day, 'Lord, it is good for us to be here!' If only we have eyes to see ...

At its best, liturgical worship ... opens our eyes not just that we might experience God in worship, but may encounter him in life.[14]

SECOND SUNDAY OF LENT (YEAR B)*

This is my Son; listen to him!

Genesis 22:1–2, 9–13, 15–18
Psalm 116:10, 15–19
Romans 8:31–34
Mark 9:2–10

Every day, children die. I used to work for a national charity that supports families bereaved through cot death. Part of my role was to work with the bereaved and to train other parents and professionals to be there for them in the hours, days, weeks, months and years of grieving that followed. For the death of a child is always devastating, whatever the cause – whether through cot death, accident, disease or illness. It is every parent's nightmare.

Death through natural causes is one thing. To be asked to give up one's child to death, voluntarily, is unthinkable. Yet that is what was demanded of Abraham when God put him to the test. The great patriarch set out, obediently, for Mount Moriah, and was at the point of striking his child, Isaac, when the angel of God intervened and a ram was offered as a sacrifice instead. No such substitute was found for another Father of another Son. For, as St Paul writes, 'He who did not withhold his own Son, but gave him up for all of us, will he not with him also give us everything else?' It is *this* Son, who now turns his face to Jerusalem and sets out upon the way of the cross, who is transfigured on the mountain before

* For readings for the Second Sunday of Lent according to the Anglican cycle, see Appendix.

Peter and James and John. It is *this* Son, the Beloved, identified and affirmed by the voice from heaven, who personifies God's call to his disciples: they are to listen to him, just as he listens to his heavenly Father. For, the Father calls and the Son obeys. Identification and command come together – both for Jesus himself and for those who hear God's voice. It is a call to obedient discipleship in the context of worship. The glory is revealed. Jesus is identified. A command is given. Yet, sometimes, following is far from easy.

For Jesus, obedience led to the cross of Calvary – the agony of separation from his friends and followers, and above all, from his heavenly Father. What might obedience mean for those who follow him? Today, we do well to remember that the cost of being an obedient disciple is one borne not only by the disciple, but by those who love him or her. Families may be divided when one or more choose to follow Christ and their choice is not respected or valued. In some cultures, such a choice will result in utter rejection and expulsion from the family home. Even Christian ministers may find that their obedience to God's call, their choosing to listen to him, alienates them from those they love and who are important to them. 'Giving things up for Lent' may be a common idea, but when it demands the giving up of those who are nearest to you, it becomes almost unthinkable. Perhaps today's readings challenge us to look at the cost from the perspective of those around us, as much as from our own? For we serve a God who gave up even his own Son.

To vow is to follow and live the incredible risk of his abandonment into our hands so many centuries ago ... In his incredible abandonment and love he depends on our capacity to love, our capacity to be faithful no matter what the cost, what the suffering. Only in his vow to us can we vow to him; in his fidelity is our faithfulness.[15]

SECOND SUNDAY OF LENT (YEAR C)*

Seek his face

Genesis 15:5–12, 17–18
Psalm 27:1, 7–9, 13–14
Philippians 3:17 – 4:1
Luke 9:28–36

We recognise people in all sorts of different ways: sometimes by reading a description of them or hearing their voice on a recording, but most commonly by seeing a picture or a photograph. Taking part in the popular party game that consists in naming famous people, whose pictures have been cut out of newspapers and magazines, can confirm for us just how important it is to know someone's face and be able to put a name to it. Faces matter. You can tell a lot about a person from their face.

In today's Gospel, we read of Jesus: 'And while he was praying, the appearance of his face changed.' Jesus prayed and his face shone. Perhaps we take this familiar phrase for granted, without remembering that, for the Jews, to look on the face of God was anathema: it was inconceivable that God should *have* a face which could be seen by mere mortals. All the more surprising, then, to read the Psalmist's words: '"Come," my heart says, "seek his face!" Your face, Lord, do I seek.' The Psalmist may have longed to see the face of God; Moses and Elijah had also longed to see God, but were prevented from doing so. For the face of God was not to be seen.

* For readings for the Second Sunday of Lent according to the Anglican cycle, see Appendix.

It was only when Jesus became a human being that what was inconceivable became a possibility; and here, on the Mount of Transfiguration, even Moses and Elijah have their long hoped-for desire fulfilled.

Seeking the face of God is, in a sense, what we do every time we pray to him and worship him. It is what you are doing now. Gazing on the one we love, and allowing that image to sink more deeply into us, is the desire of every lover – both human and divine. We can 'seek the face of God' in a whole variety of ways: in reflecting on the words of Scripture, in agonising over the troubles of our world which we see displayed on our TV screens each day, in trying to live lives that genuinely seek to respond to his calling at every moment. Yet, surely, one of the most obvious ways in which we can seek the face of God is to look for him in our fellow human beings. They are made in his image just as much as we are. As we reflect on the face of God in prayer and study, so our faces become enlightened, envisioned with his, and others will begin to see his image in us. But we also have our eyes opened to see his face in others. To live this way transforms discipleship. God's invitation to us, this Lent, is both to ascend the mountain and descend from it again – to see the vision and listen to his voice, and then see and hear the same Transfigured One in the faces and voices of his beloved children.

The vision of Christ is the transfiguration of man (sic).[16]

MONDAY IN WEEK 2

Skirting the issue

Daniel 9:4–10
Psalm 79:8–9, 11, 13
Luke 6:36–38

In his book of reflections on St Luke's Gospel, chapter 15, Kenneth E. Bailey[17] vividly describes the father of the prodigal hitching up his skirts and running through the streets of the town to greet his wayward son as he returns home. It is a picture that is both delightful and shocking, for it not only speaks of the father's exhilaration, but also breaks all the rules and runs completely counter to the cultural expectations of a refined head of a Jewish household.

The Psalmist paints a similarly vivid image as he pleads with God to be merciful towards Jerusalem, a city brought to a state of dereliction by the nations round about. 'Let your compassion come speedily to meet us,' he writes, conscious of the shame, the mocking and the suffering that Zion and its inhabitants have endured – however justified their treatment may have been. In a similar way, the prophet Daniel pleads on behalf of his fellow Jews, held captive in Babylon – confessing the corporate failings of the disparate nation and affirming – for his own sake as much as theirs – the mercy and forgiveness of God: 'To the Lord our God belong mercy and forgiveness, for we have rebelled against him ...' Two things, then, are particularly striking from today's readings. First, the image of a compassionate and merciful God who longs for his people's return. Second, the role of a community's leaders in being ready to plead and make confession on their behalf.

The season of Lent certainly serves to focus our awareness of our need for forgiveness: through the Scriptures, through personal reflection and abstinence, through the often more austere nature of our corporate worship. But how well do we balance that austerity with a focus on the God who longs, with deep compassion, for our return? Are we good at recognising our sinfulness and blind to the loving-kindness and mercy that is there to greet it? Christian ministers play a key role in presenting this balance. Not only are we to encourage individuals to take seriously their personal Lenten disciplines, we are also to encourage a corporate reflection on the worshipping community's relationship with God. As we do, we will both enable the merciful and generous living that Luke commends, as well as encourage the community of disciples to seek forgiveness and a new start. Yet, even this is not enough, for it ignores the most powerful and vital dimension to the whole equation. That is, the delightful and shocking truth that, despite all our failings, we have a God who, apparently, breaks all the rules, 'hitches up his skirts' and longs to come out to meet us.

God lays every thing aside, that he may serve his servants; heaven stoops to earth, and one abyss calls upon another, and the miseries of man, which were next to infinite, are excelled by a mercy equal to the immensity of God.[18]

TUESDAY IN WEEK 2

Practise what you preach

Isaiah 1:10, 16–20
Psalm 50:8, 16–end
Matthew 23:1–12

I used to teach in a theological college. One of the courses I contributed to was the Preaching Course, and I usually worked with small groups of students who had some limited experience of preaching, but who were basically starting from scratch. So where did we begin? One of the first things I used to talk about was concerning the *attitude* with which one approached the task. Most of the students were pretty nervous about the whole idea; but dealing with nerves was not what I focused on. It was more to do with how the person preaching and the sermon preached, connected. Some students were very concerned to *understand* the text; I used to begin by encouraging them to *stand under* the text, by which I meant that they should allow the passage or passages of Scripture to speak to *them* first, before ever considering the possibility of speaking to others. Perhaps it is an obvious place to start – but, so often, it is not.

Jesus' words in today's Gospel, addressed to the crowds and to his disciples, are blunt: 'Do whatever they teach you and follow it; but do not do as they do ...' The scribes and Pharisees were saying all the right things, but their lives demonstrated something that was poles apart: their words lacked integrity, because what they said with their lips, they appeared *not* to believe in their hearts. The Psalmist recognises a similar problem: the wicked have aroused the wrath of

God's judgement because, says God: 'you hate discipline, and ... cast my words behind you.' One moment they are reciting the statutes; in another, they are lying and slandering even their own families. Pronouncing the message is one thing; living the life is another.

Those who are called to preach the word of God to others hold a special responsibility to first preach it to themselves. So often sermons are written at the last minute, or not even *written* at all. The pressures of a wider ministry can easily eat away at time needed for preparation; for many ministers, it is a perennial problem. Yet, even when there is little time for *writing*, there needs to be plenty of time for prayerful reflection – the 'taking in' of the word of God – its 'inwardly digesting' as Cranmer's well-known collect for Bible Sunday puts it – so that the preacher's life is changed by it, as deeply as the lives of those to whom the message is preached. We need constantly to *stand under* as well as *understand*. And it's not just a message for preachers: disciples who do not preach from pulpits or lecterns are as susceptible as those who do. For all of us preach with our lives, even if we don't with our words.

The character of [the preacher's] Sermon is Holiness ... It is gained ... by dipping, and seasoning all our words and sentences in our hearts, before they come into our mouths, truly affecting, and cordially expressing all that we say; so that the auditors may plainly perceive that every word is heart-deep.[19]

WEDNESDAY IN WEEK 2

Ambivalent ambition

Jeremiah 18:18–20
Psalm 31:4–5, 13–18
Mathew 20:17–28

'The trouble is', he said, as the tears began to flow down his cheeks, 'I always wanted to be a bishop, and nobody asked me ...' Patrick had done all the right things: he'd been to the right theological college and the right curacy; served in the right parishes and on all the right committees; he'd got to know all the right people and said all the right things – but somehow it had never happened. And here he was, at sixty-one, finally admitting to himself what others had known for a long time: that he would complete his ministerial service as a parish priest. It was a painful realisation.

Consciousness of status, and the recognition that it may not be as secure as it should, is a common thread through today's readings. Jeremiah – hounded by the people, who are (understandably) sick and tired of his tirades against them – complains to God that the treatment he's receiving doesn't correspond to the service he has rendered. The Psalmist is under severe pressure from those around. And the Sons of Thunder seem quite happy to collude with their ambitious mother's request, in spite of what it might cost them, because status was all-important. Yet they would pay the price with their lives.

Jesus' well-known words from today's Gospel, 'It will not be so among you', come as a challenge to many Christian leaders who secretly, or openly, cherish an ambition to become 'great' in the kingdom of heaven. Yet, sometimes, their understanding of greatness is more akin to that of the 'rulers of the Gentiles' than the King of the Jews. Others are very clear that this is not a right way to think or behave: they should not seek preferment or promotion or even look for recognition at all: service is what it should all be about – and they are right. There seems to be an ambivalence about ambition that means they hide and do nothing; but so often, secretly, even these find themselves (like the other disciples) looking on angrily at those who are climbing the greasy pole.

As with so many things, the problem lies not with status or greatness in itself, but with the attitude towards it. There will always be great Christian leaders. There will always be those who hold authority over others. There will always be those who prosper and for whom everything seems to work out well. Yet those who *seek after* greatness fool themselves and have missed the point. For, the way to greatness in the kingdom of heaven is the way of service and trust, and ultimately the way of the cross. The difference between James and John and Jesus is that *they* tried to make it happen. He allowed it to happen *to* him – with *all* that it cost.

Thou art God; no monarch thou
Thron'd in easy state to reign;
Thou art God, Whose arms of love
Aching, spent, the world sustain.[20]

THURSDAY IN WEEK 2

Nil by mouth

Jeremiah 17:5–10
Psalm 1
Luke 16:19–end

When someone is seriously ill, following a stroke or accident or heart attack, or when they are awaiting a major operation, the sign 'Nil by mouth' is often placed above their bed. Those who have experienced, or witnessed such a situation will know the acute discomfort it brings: swallowing becomes difficult, if not impossible; speech is not easy and the lips and tongue become parched, distended and dry. Life is sustained intravenously, as drips provide water and liquid nourishment to the patient, who would otherwise rapidly dehydrate and die.

The images of trees by rivers in the desert that we find in today's Psalm and Old Testament reading are not dissimilar – a 'natural world' version, perhaps, of 'nil by mouth'. The rains have ceased, the wind is blowing and those who trust in the Lord and walk in his way have their roots directed to the ever-flowing stream. Even in the heat of the desert and the year of drought, those trees continue to have green leaves and bear fruit. They survive under pressure because the source of life keeps flowing. The rich man in today's parable from Luke's Gospel also knows the discomfort of 'nil by mouth': but his request to Father Abraham for Lazarus to come and 'dip the tip of his finger in water and cool my tongue' is refused. For the rich man has had his chance in life, and has missed it. He has selfishly enjoyed his home comforts and taken little notice of those who suffer on his doorstep. Moreover, until now, he has taken even less notice of God himself.

Today's readings remind us of the necessity of a steady and trusting relationship with the Lord that is nurtured and maintained by giving regular attention to his word. Those who are ordained are encouraged by the bishop at their ordination to 'pray that [God] will each day enlarge and enlighten your understanding of the Scriptures', and they undertake to say the daily offices as part of their personal and corporate discipline. Many lay people also have a rule of life that includes the saying of an office and meditating on a portion of Scripture each day. As such they become like 'trees planted by streams of water' and, so often, the value of such a discipline only really becomes clear when the sun beats down, the desert wind blows and life feels like an 'uninhabited salt land'.

The parable of the rich man and Lazarus warns us never to take our present comfort and stability for granted. Instead, we are to observe God's word *now* – when things are good. We are to put out roots that will nourish us when pressure comes. We are to trust that when *we* face situations of 'nil by mouth' (actual or metaphorical), not only will life be maintained, intravenously, but we will also continue to bear fruit for our gracious God.

The desert does not allow any compromise. **(A monk)**[21]

FRIDAY IN WEEK 2

Rejected!

Genesis 37:3–4, 12–13, 17–28
Psalm 105:16–22
Matthew 21:33–43, 45–46

All the letter said was that the elders of the church had come to a unanimous decision that Terence should be asked to leave: he was no longer the minister they wanted. He was devastated. He believed that God had called him to this church; he had a vision for it and he was working hard to turn vision into reality. He had (he believed) preached faithfully to them of their need to change and grow – the necessity to develop a radical edge to their Gospel ministry. Now they were telling him they didn't want him, and would he and his family kindly pack their bags and vacate the manse by the end of the year.

Those who are called and sent by God often have a rough ride. Joseph must have wondered what he had done when his brothers first threw him into a pit and then sold him as a slave to an Ishmaelite caravan en route to Egypt. He must have wondered even more when he was wrongfully arrested and thrown into an Egyptian jail. But then things started to get better, and the man whom God had 'sent ahead' became the saviour of his people when they fled to Egypt because of the famine. Joseph's problem was that he was a man of vision, and he wasn't afraid to speak out; but his brothers couldn't cope with his 'dreams' and the arrogance that went with them, and so they rejected him and sent him on his way.

Visionary leadership is not always welcome in the Christian

community. It can threaten both people and plans. It can seem to undermine what is already happening and question the validity of what people hold dear. It can cause jealousy, conflict, resentment – even hatred and division – and people can be hurt and bruised and crushed because of it. The ministers themselves can be far from perfect in the way they go about things, risking arrogance, pomposity and abuse of power. Yet none of this takes away the pain, when those they have been serving, turn around and say, 'Sorry. We don't want you any more.'

All of us share a responsibility to pray for those who serve the Christian community in leadership. Most ministers will have experienced rejection of their ministry to some degree or another: it is part of the risk of service. Few, however, will have been asked to leave their jobs because their message is too radical, too demanding. Perhaps the parable of the wicked tenants from Matthew's Gospel is a healthy reminder to all of us of the possibility of rejection, and the cost of ministry to those who are faithful to the owner of the vineyard. For some, it will cost them their lives. What matters is that we remain faithful to the God who calls and willing to trust him when things are going wrong. The likelihood is that it is all part of his bigger purposes – just as it was for Joseph, and for the Son of God himself.

God, who is everywhere, never leaves us. Yet, He seems sometimes to be present, sometimes absent. If we do not know Him well, we do not realise that He may be more present to us when He is absent than when He is present.[22]

SATURDAY IN WEEK 2

Restoration

Micah 7:14–15, 18–20
Psalm 103:1–4, 9–12
Luke 15:1–3, 11–end

In recent decades in the UK, there has been a resurgence of interest in our historic roots and the heritage we enjoy in ancient sites and buildings. This has been focused, recently, in the popularity of a television series called *Restoration.* Crumbling edifices are visited, assessed and offered to a voting public as worthy of renovation, and one lucky building is chosen to receive ample funding for the work to be completed and the structure to be made whole. In many cases, the aim is not only to 'save' the construction, but also to bring back to life the activity or enterprise for which it was originally built: there is to be resurrection as well as restoration.

Today's readings are not about buildings in need of restoration: they are about lives. The Psalmist's whole being overflows with joy at the goodness of the God who forgives, heals and redeems his people and crowns them 'with steadfast love and mercy'. Here is a God who does not harbour anger or accusation; here is a God whose mercy is not measured; here is a God whose love for his people is so immense that even the circumference of the world is not sufficient to distance their sinfulness from them. And the prophet Micah rejoices in the same truth as he cries out: 'You will cast all our sins into the depths of the sea.' Reading this alongside the narrative of the prodigal's return, we are left in no doubt about the extent of God's pardon and the vastness of his love.

Yet, we sometimes live as if this were not so. God is wholehearted in his forgiveness of those who return to him in repentance and faith. There is no shadow of turning; no 'ifs', no 'buts' – just open arms and a warm embrace. I sometimes wonder whether the same can be said about the Church of God? Do we *really* welcome the sinners and tax collectors of our own age? Do we *really* welcome back those who have plundered our wealth and our generosity and yet come back for more? Or are we like the Pharisees and the scribes who grumble at God's mercy and are affronted by his compassion towards those they hold in disdain?

Only when we learn again to love the crumbling edifices of our own lives – and recognise our own need of restoration, will we truly be able to rejoice in the new life he gives to others. Only when we learn again to accept our own sinfulness and need of redemption, will we be able to echo the Psalmist's words: 'Bless the Lord, O my soul, and *all* that is within me, bless his holy name.'

The Church is the trustee of the gospel of redemption: and unless the gospel is preached, the Church is not the Church.[23]

THIRD WEEK OF LENT

Take up thy cross; nor heed the shame,
Nor let thy foolish pride rebel;
The Lord for thee the Cross endured,
To save thy soul from death and hell.

THIRD SUNDAY OF LENT (YEAR A)

Taking the flak

Exodus 17:1–7
Psalm 95
Romans 5:1–11
John 4:5–42

Negotiations had reached a very delicate stage. The key independent sponsor was threatening to withdraw its funding from the project because members of other faith communities were not going to be allowed to use the new church and community centre. Susan, the vicar, felt caught. The local authority was encouraging the development of multipurpose buildings as part of its strategy for community integration. The PCC were adamant that the new church centre was for use by 'Christians' only. Susan was playing 'piggy-in-the-middle' – receiving the flak from both sides.

Moses must have been under a similar sort of pressure. God was commanding him to lead the people of Israel through the wilderness by stages; the people were protesting that, where they had been told to set up camp, there was no water to drink. It was a legitimate complaint. The result was a stand-off between the people and God. They complained at Moses; God complained about them. And Moses was caught in the middle. So he cried out in desolation to the Lord: 'What shall I do with this people?' Desperation led to prayer, which, in turn, led to a way forward. God, we read, 'went ahead' of Moses (who was accompanied by some of the elders), to the rock at Horeb, and as Moses obeyed the Lord's instruction and struck the rock with his staff, so water gushed from the rock and the people's thirst was quenched. But he had had to live with the discomfort of standing in the middle and taking the flak.

The experience of Susan and Moses is not uncommon. It may not be about building new church centres or finding water for a nomadic people, but there will often be circumstances – personal and strategic – where ministers find themselves bearing the brunt of frustration and complaints. Criticism and quarrels proliferate; and very often people look for tangible proof that their views have been noted. It can be acutely wearing, and like Moses, the cry, 'What shall I do with this people?' may not be far from a leader's lips. Taking the flak seems to go with the territory.

Perhaps, when the pressure is on, Paul's letter to the Romans has something to offer us. For here we see afresh that, in Christ, God has 'gone ahead' of us in every way. It is through him that 'we have obtained access to the grace in which we stand', a grace dependent not on *us*, but solely on God's love. And we stand in it now. Suffering, endurance and character may be the outcome of 'taking the flak'. Yet, the one who caused water to gush from a rock, and who, in Christ, gives the living water that leads to eternal life, also gives to his servants, through the Holy Spirit, a hope that does not disappoint. He has gone ahead of us at every stage. In the midst of conflict and tension, this is, surely, a promise worth remembering.

God can do everything and I can do nothing. But if I offer this nothing in prayer to God, everything becomes possible in me.[24]

THIRD SUNDAY OF LENT (YEAR B)

Simple wisdom

Exodus 20:1–17
Psalm 19:7–end
1 Corinthians 1:18–25
John 2:13–25

When I was a university chaplain, one of the tasks at the beginning of each academic year was to accompany the dean and various other members of staff in introducing the life of the community to the new first years. 'College Regulations' always featured in the dean's talk. Basically, he would say, everything you need to know about how to make this community function smoothly and effectively is contained in this book. I sometimes wonder how many undergraduates actually read them! Beyond the walls of the institution, rules and regulations are given so that life is manageable for everyone. Just imagine what it would be like if there were no Highway Code; no rules governing matters of employment, education, health and safety or transport; no planning regulations restricting building in inappropriate locations. The trouble with rules (as membership of the European Union so amply illustrates) is that they can become so complex that we lose sight of what they are there for – which is to help human beings live together peaceably in community. Ultimately, rules exist for the sake of relationships.

One of the benefits of the Jewish Law (according to the Psalmist) is that it both revives the soul and makes wise the simple. We are told that it also brings joy to the heart and insight into the ways of God. Clearly, like 'College

Regulations', the Law was given primarily to enable the people of God to live together peaceably, in the fear of the Lord. By the time Jesus stormed the Temple in Jerusalem, turning the tables and driving out the money-changers, the Law had become a straitjacket and a distraction to meaningful and lively relationships both with God and neighbour. One of the reasons, surely, that Jesus was so angry in the Temple was that the rules relating to sacrifices of animals had become so important – commercially as well as spiritually – that people were more concerned about buying the right combination of doves and goats than they were about worshipping the God of Israel. The sheer complexity of the Law was such that it left people feeling trapped and condemned by their frequent failure to obey. Simple wisdom, it seems, was not enough.

It is much easier, in many ways, to preach a gospel of rules than a gospel of love. Indeed, the Church has so often mirrored the complexity of its Jewish forebears by burdening people with a baggage of 'oughts' and 'musts' that would have rejoiced the heart of many a Pharisee. So often, as one theologian has put it, we find ourselves bound by the imperatives of the Law rather than freed by the indicatives of grace. Jesus' message to the Pharisees was simple. If they needed a sign to prove who he was, he would give them the sign of his own body – crucified on a cross and raised to life after three days, and all for love. It was, to Jew and Greek, a stumbling block – complete and utter foolishness. Yet this is the simple wisdom we are called to proclaim.

The Christian, whatever his understanding may be in other matters, is wise in respect of his end, which is the main point of wisdom.[25]

THIRD SUNDAY OF LENT (YEAR C)*

Turn aside and take off your shoes

Exodus 3:1–8, 13–15
Psalm 103:1–11
1 Corinthians 10:1–13
Luke 13:1–9

Each day, I walk across Palace Green on my way to the early Eucharist at Ely Cathedral. Each day, whatever the weather, I am struck once more by the immense grandeur of this noble and gracious edifice and the greatness of the God in whose honour it was built. The sense of awe continues as I enter the west door and make my way up the nave to whichever chapel is being used for the celebration that day. It is a special place and I hope I will never take it for granted.

When Moses encounters the burning bush, on the far side of the wilderness, it is curiosity that first draws him: 'I must turn aside and look at this strange sight', he says. Yet, as soon as God calls to him by name, he begins to recognise the sanctity of the moment and the holiness of the one who is calling him. 'Remove the sandals from your feet', says God, and so follows Moses' great commission to lead God's people out of slavery. Today's Epistle and Gospel, each in their different ways, also encourage us not to take things for granted. St Paul is direct in his warning to the Corinthians. They are not to be like the 'wicked' people of Israel – always moaning and complaining, in spite of God's care for them.

* In the Anglican cycle, the Old Testament reading for today is Isaiah 55:1–9 and the Psalm is 63:1–8.

Neither is there to be any room for complacency: 'So if you think you are standing, watch out that you do not fall.' Similarly, Jesus' words to his followers about the Galileans and the victims of the Tower of Siloam disaster, make it quite plain that God does not distinguish between bad sinners and 'not so bad' sinners: 'Unless you repent, you will all perish just as they did.'

Today, our readings urge us again to be awe-struck by the holiness of God and not to be complacent. It is not always easy. We may not have access to an awe-inspiring building in which to worship. We may be snowed under with the regular demands of any Sunday – preparations for church, getting lunch ready, looking after family needs and so on. There are always more pressing things to do than to 'turn aside', as Moses did, and encounter God. And yet it is in the 'turning aside' – even for a moment – that we give God permission (as it were) to call us by name again, and to invite us to remove the sandals from our feet. If we do not encounter his holiness, then we will risk becoming complacent about our own needs and failings – just as the Corinthians were in danger of doing. But when we *do* – even if only out of curiosity – then we will recognise our need of repentance and rejoice, with the Psalmist that, 'As the heavens are high above the earth, so great is his steadfast love toward those who fear him.'

Our sins and vices are grounds for rightful sorrow and contrition of heart; for they have so strong a hold on us that we are seldom able to contemplate heavenly things.[26]

MONDAY IN WEEK 3

Unlikely messenger, unlikely message

2 Kings 5:1–15
Psalms 42:1–2; 43:1–4
Luke 4:24–30

One hundred and fifty years ago, Tom would have been known as the 'village idiot'. Simple but harmless. People knew him as part of the community, but they couldn't take him seriously: he was just there, often to be seen wandering up and down the village street, bouncing a ball or singing nursery rhymes to himself – just as he had since childhood. So when he turned up at the vicarage one Christmas Eve, and said he had found baby Jesus in the churchyard, no one quite believed him; seasonal excitement had obviously allowed this forty-year-old's childish imagination to run riot. Tom was insistent, however, and just to placate him, the vicar went with him; at least he would have the chance to tell him the Christmas story again and show him the crib in church. Imagine how shocked he was to discover an abandoned infant, wrapped in a blanket in a cardboard box, propped up against a gravestone ... Tom was an unlikely messenger, with an unlikely, but important, message.

There are several messengers and messages in today's Old Testament reading: a foreign servant-girl speaks to her mistress, who speaks to her husband, who speaks to the King of Aram, who sends a letter, with a delegation, to the King of Israel asking for healing for his great commander Naaman. Then there is the prophet who sends a message to the King, who sends Naaman to Elisha, who sends a messenger to

Naaman (with an unlikely request) – who is affronted and goes off in a huff. Finally, there are the servants who gently reproach their master for his pride and whose courage makes possible the healing Naaman sought. Foreigners and servants taking risks to bring about the purposes of God. Unlikely messages passed on to others, so that God's will might be fulfilled.

In most communities, there are people we expect to take the lead: the parish councillors, the head of the local primary school, the GP, the vicar, the local MP. They are the ones who speak to and for the community – the 'establishment', the ones who know the score and who have the wisdom and goodwill to try to help the community flourish. And the church community is no different: there are the elders, the deacons, the clergy, the members of the church council – all of whom have the good of the community at heart and who seek to be bearers of 'good news' to those around them. Occasionally, however, God uses unlikely messengers, who bring unlikely (sometimes unwanted) messages – and whose words sometimes go unheard because *who they are* and *what they say* doesn't fit with the expectations of those who should be listening. And the reaction can be strong – as Jesus himself discovered at the synagogue in Nazareth.

Perhaps today is a day for looking and listening out for the unlikely – but courageous – messenger from God. For the unusual message they bring might be *just* what we need to hear ...

If we knew how to listen to God, we should hear him speaking to us. For God does speak. He speaks in his Gospel; he speaks also through life ... But because our faith is too weak and our life too earth-bound, we are rarely open to God's message.[27]

TUESDAY IN WEEK 3

Give as good as you get

Song of the Three 2, 11–20*
Psalm 25:3–10
Matthew 18:21–35

The pattern of reprisal and revenge attacks, evidence of decades of conflict in the Middle East and Northern Ireland, is one with which we are all too familiar. We no longer notice, it seems. 'Tit for tat' is the name of the game; and what we accept all too easily as we listen to the news, surreptitiously becomes part of our personal and church agendas. 'If he treats me with contempt, then I'll do the same ...' 'If she makes a fool of me in public, then I'll embarrass her too ...' Perhaps, as Christians, we are quick to deny the charge – but perhaps not; for, sadly, the Christian Church can be as much a hotbed of ill feeling, bad behaviour and lack of forgiveness as any secular context. On the larger scale, factions of the Church make statements about truth and argue via the Letters column of *The Times*; bishops and other Church leaders are slandered and accusations made of heresy and dissent. At a personal level, things are said or done, people are hurt and relationships are broken. Forgiveness and mercy can seem a very long way away.

Into this, Jesus says, 'You wicked slave! I forgave you all that debt ... Should you not have had mercy ... as I had mercy on you?' Despite its treatment by the media, those outside the Church might be excused for imagining that relationships

* In the Anglican cycle the Old Testament reading is Daniel 2:20–23.

among a community of believers must be healthy and blameless: those within the Church are painfully aware that sometimes this is far from the truth. Forgiveness and mercy are needed here, just as much as in Jerusalem or Belfast. Today's readings help us to reflect on the frailty of being human and the constant tendency to veer from God's way, and to follow a path of retribution, blame and bitterness rather than the path of righteousness. The parable of the unforgiving servant tells us that we are to 'give as good as we get' – but not in the way the world understands that phrase. Rather we are to offer mercy and forgiveness to others, just as we ourselves have been granted mercy and forgiveness by our heavenly Father.

Those who lead any Christian community can be aware of long-running and unresolved disputes – both on the large scale and between individuals. They themselves may even be caught up in them. The good news, as both the Psalmist and Daniel remind us, is that God already *knows* our failings: 'He knows what is in the darkness and light dwells with him', and he longs to lead us in his paths – especially those of us who have strayed, and who acknowledge that we are humble and poor. Being prepared to forgive others *from the heart* and lead others to forgive is part of our calling; but we must start with ourselves – and give as good as *we* get, from him who loved us and gave his life as a ransom for many.

[The Son] gives us a declaration of free forgiveness ... it is free in that we could never make any beginning of earning it, and can only receive it from Him as a gift. But in another sense it is not free ... It is that as we wish to be forgiven, so we shall forgive.[28]

WEDNESDAY IN WEEK 3

Beyond the letter of the law

Deuteronomy 4:1, 5–9
Psalm 147:12–end
Matthew 5:17–19

We live in an increasingly legalistic and litigious society. Rules, regulations and rights can tend to dominate the thinking of governments, businesses and organisations. Ministers and leaders in every context find themselves ever more bound by the requirements of European, federal or global legislation, in respect of a wide range of environmental, employment and human rights issues: and the Church is not exempt. More and more time and energy has to be spent on dealing with the legal dimensions of the work in which we are involved: health and safety, disability legislation, employment law, criminal records checks, to name a few – all matters of significance and importance. Yet, who can blame those who have a sense that it is all a time-consuming, if necessary, distraction? Who can blame those who wonder, from time to time, what it is all *for*?

When Moses exhorted the people of Israel to 'give heed to the statutes and ordinances that I am teaching you to observe,' he was setting a pattern that they were to continue long after he had left them. The law was to be taught from generation to generation – a practice that continues to this day in orthodox Jewish homes. Not only that, the teaching and keeping of the law was to be something that would help the community to function more peacefully – something that other nations would remark upon with envy, causing them to exclaim: 'Surely this great nation is a wise and discerning people!' The law was to be viewed as a positive, creative and necessary component of the life of the nation. Nevertheless, it was not just to be a matter of knowing and keeping the *letter* of the law; *experience* was to play a part also. The people had seen the majesty of God at Horeb: they were to remember that experience and it was to be part of the story they passed on. The law was not an end in itself, but a means to maintaining a right relationship with God and with their fellow human beings from one generation to another. They had to look *beyond* the letter to what the law was for.

Jesus' teaching in the Sermon on the Mount makes the same point. The law of Moses is necessary and good, he says – but there is more to it than that. For the law exists not to suppress or oppress, but to create an environment in which love may be expressed in action – an environment where people experience afresh the majesty and grace of God and the wise and discerning actions of God's people. When this happens, love becomes truly the fulfilling of the law.

It is tempting to think that completing the latest pile of forms about health and safety is a waste of a minister's time. Perhaps that is the moment to think beyond the letter of the law to the love that fulfils it.

We must love because God hath so commanded, and because it is the fulfilling of all his commandments.[29]

THURSDAY IN WEEK 3

Listen to his voice

Jeremiah 7:23–28
Psalm 95:1–2, 6–end
Luke 11:14–23

Half way through Lent, and perhaps it's getting tough? Ash Wednesday seems a long time ago, Easter Day an aeon away. There's Holy Week to prepare for: palm crosses to order, meditations to write, and the new Paschal candle hasn't yet arrived. This week's Lent speaker has cried off sick and the person organising the hunger lunches can't be there today, so you've got to remember to put the soup on. The other church leaders don't seem to be pulling their weight in preparing for the agape service and you feel you've got to make all the ecumenical running for yet another year. Somehow, it's more difficult than ever to keep time and space for yourself and for God ... And a little voice inside says, 'Why bother? You've got more than enough to do ...'

Into the midst of all this, today's readings come as a reminder that *this* is what we are to do: we are to listen to his voice. But it's not easy. The people of Israel found it extraordinarily difficult: they hardened their hearts, looked for signs to prove that God was God, stubbornly turned their backs on him and shut their ears to his word. They ignored his messengers and did their own thing – even when the messengers tried to alert them to their fate. And the result? They found they could no longer hear or speak the truth: 'Truth has perished; it is cut off from their lips.' Like some of the crowd who witnessed the healing of the dumb man, they could no longer recognise God at work in their midst.

What was true for the people of Israel can be true for us also. It is easy for hearts to be hardened by pressure of work. It is easy for backs to be turned – oh, so subtly – on the God who longs for us to see him face to face. It is easy for ears to be shut to his message of love and grace and comfort. It is easy for truth to perish and for the kingdom of God to risk being divided against itself as communications falter and resentments build. To read today's Psalm may be, for many of us, an act of the will. Yet its invitation to us to offer our worship to God our rock – a God before whom we are invited to kneel, to bow down and to incline our ear – is an invitation he will offer again and again and again. Especially when we're being stubborn.

'O that today you would listen to his voice!'

But as I rav'd and grew more fierce and wild
At every word
Me thought I heard one calling, 'Child':
And I replied, 'My Lord.'[30]

FRIDAY IN WEEK 3

With all your heart

Hosea 14:2–10
Psalm 81:6–10, 13, 16
Mark 12:28–34

Falling in love can be a dangerous business – especially for those in the public eye. For when you are in love with someone, you can become almost completely preoccupied with a yearning to be with them, to see them, listen to them, laugh with them, touch them and know their every longing and desire. Their hopes and joys become yours; their losses and pains also. When they hurt you, you long to forgive; and when you hurt them, you long to be forgiven. Falling in love demands the whole of you – heart, soul, mind and strength – and the pain of losing one you love demands even more. But falling in love is only ever part of the story ...

There is one phrase that is common to both of today's readings: it is the phrase 'with all my/your heart'. In Hosea, it is the measure of God's love for his people; in Mark it is to *be* the measure of our love for God. It is extravagant, intense, excessive; irrepressible, passionate, unending. It is a love that identifies completely with the other, and it is a love that does not fade. Yet it is also steady – *steadfast* as Scripture puts it – a love built as much on a foundation of the will as on the emotions; a love that is sometimes a matter of choice rather than inclination. 'Falling in love' has, somehow, deepened into 'being in love'.

Most of us reflect on such things and feel woefully inadequate: what may be true of God, is surely not true of us –

either in terms of our love for God himself, or of our love for one another. Our passions are fickle, our love sporadic at best. Perhaps that is why the second part of the Great Commandment (as it is known) is so important: 'You shall love your neighbour as yourself.' For it is in and through the steady love of our neighbour that we may both give and receive the love of the God who loves us with all his heart. Many of us find the demands of this second directive even more impossible than the first. Not because we do not want to love our neighbour; far from it! No, we find it impossible because we do not want to love *ourselves*. We want to give and give and give, without return. A laudable desire at face value, perhaps? Yet, if God longs for us to love *him* with all that we are, then who are we to think we can manage on any less? Indeed, resisting the love of God may even be deemed to be sinful. Here, then, is the real sticking point for so many of us: love is not just about our capacity to love God or our neighbour with all *our* heart; rather it is about allowing ourselves to love *ourselves*, and to *be loved* with all *his* heart.

Who will you allow to love you today?

No created being can comprehend how much, and how sweetly, and how tenderly our maker loves us.[31]

SATURDAY IN WEEK 3

Know yourself

Hosea 5:15 – 6:6
Psalm 51:1–2, 17–end
Luke 18:9–14

One of the tasks for Christian ministers is to be aware of the spiritual and personal growth and development of those in their care – both individuals and the community as a whole. Knowing the flock is a pre-requisite to feeding and guiding them and it is this awareness, attained through careful listening and effective pastoral care, that shapes the teaching and nurturing roles that are also part of a minister's responsibility. Inevitably, judgements about others must be made. Who has the spiritual depth to lead intercessions? Who has the capacity to develop a pastoral ministry themselves? Who has the biblical knowledge to be entrusted with leading a study group? It is a necessary part of a minister's calling.

But there is a 'flip-side' to this ability – as our Gospel reading makes plain: for it must be matched by an appropriate self-awareness and a sober estimate of one's own gifts, abilities and standing before God. To all outward appearances, the Pharisee was the 'religious' professional – the one who did all the right things, kept all the rules; the one who confidently stood by himself in the public place, praying his prayers out loud for all to hear. Surely *he* was the sort of person who would be approved and chosen by God? By contrast, the tax collector stood afar off, condemned as a collaborator, praying quietly, repentant, with his eyes cast down, unnoticed by the crowd. Surely *he* was *not* the sort God would choose?

Two strands for reflection emerge from our readings today. First, when we choose people to take on leadership roles in the Christian community, do we discern those whom *God* would choose, or simply the ones who 'stand out' and speak loudest? Do we need constantly, rather, to be searching among the shadows of the worshipping community to discover the ones who truly know their need of God, and who may therefore have more to give? Second, do we really know *ourselves*, or is our estimate of ourselves greater than it should be? Do we hide behind the confident exterior of our public role, not even recognising, let alone acknowledging, the emptiness that may be within? Are we especially prone to comparing ourselves with other Christian leaders – thinking we are better than they, and regarding them with contempt?

Admitting the possibility that we may be more like the Pharisee than the tax collector is the first step to a deeper self-knowledge and to receiving the mercy and grace of God. It is also the way to see more clearly the humble gifts of those who go unnoticed. Yet, like the people of Israel, we have to acknowledge our guilt and turn back to God, before we can begin to know his healing and feel the refreshing, cleansing spring rains of his love.

... Man, proud man,
Drest in a little brief authority,
Most ignorant of what he's most assured,
His glassy essence, like an angry ape,
Plays such fantastic tricks before high heaven
As make the angels weep; who, with our spleens,
Would all themselves laugh mortal.[32]

FOURTH WEEK OF LENT

Take up thy cross then in his strength,
And calmly every danger brave;
'Twill guide thee to a better home,
And lead to victory o'er the grave.

FOURTH SUNDAY OF LENT (YEAR A)

Now you see it, now you don't

1 Samuel 16:1–13
Psalm 23
Ephesians 5:8–14
John 9:1–41

Puzzle books and quizzes are enjoying a revival. There can be something rather stimulating and energising about the sorts of brain-teasers that appear in countless books, on countless shelves, in countless bookstores shortly before Christmas. Many people also seem to enjoy 'sitting in' on such TV favourites as *The Weakest Link* and *Who Wants to be a Millionaire?* We seem to like the challenge of asking and answering questions; and we like to get the answers right. A few years ago, a game called 'Dingbats' was particularly popular. In it, a range of visual patterns or words or shapes were offered to the players, designed to prompt them to come up with a well-known phrase or saying or proverb. For some, the answer was obvious straight away; for others, try as they might, they could not get beyond the surface to see – with insight – what the strange combination of lines and letters might mean.

The story of the healing of the man born blind from today's Gospel reading might well be described as a series of 'dingbats': time and again, people in the story are shown something, or told something, but they cannot perceive what is going on. There is, it seems, sight, but no insight. The disciples assume, wrongly, that the man's blindness is caused by sin. The neighbours struggle to come to terms with the transformation from blind beggar to witnessing disciple. The Pharisees persist in asking the man to tell his story, trying to find an explanation for his cure that will not contradict their expectations of how, and through whom, God works; they cross-question his parents and then turn again on the blind man himself in a way that would surely have aggravated the Police Complaints Commission were it to have existed at the time! It seems that however plainly the blind man states his case, the Pharisees cannot 'see' the simple truth that he has been healed by Jesus Christ. He even asks them if *they* want to become disciples – they seem so interested in him!

It is a story with infinite layers of meaning, but for those who are leaders in the community, there are perhaps two insights to take away and ponder during the course of today: one, an encouragement, the other, a warning. For this passage demonstrates, amply, the fact that, when it comes to matters of belief, what is obvious to some is hidden from others; there will be those who see and believe – even if they don't understand; and there will be others who seem never to cease to question, and who will look for every kind of explanation, rather than accept the power of God at work among them. We are called to love and work with them all, but we cannot make them 'see'. Only *God* can. More penetratingly, the passage also reminds us that it is those who *think* they know how God works, who are sometimes the most blind and the most taken by surprise.

By our own powers we cannot see God, yet God will be seen by us because he wills it. He will be seen by those he chooses at the time he chooses, and in the way he chooses, for God can do all things.[33]

FOURTH SUNDAY OF LENT (YEAR B)*

God's work of art

2 Chronicles 36:14–16, 19–23
Psalm 137:1–6
Ephesians 2:1–10
John 3:14–21

One of the longest running disputes in the history of art concerns the Elgin (or Parthenon) Marbles. 'Stolen' from Greece at the turn of the nineteenth century, by the ambassador to the Ottoman Empire, Thomas Bruce, the Seventh Earl of Elgin, they have remained in the British Museum in London since the early 1800s: works of art, in a strange land. Understandably, the Greek government has, on many occasions, requested their repatriation on the grounds that they should be re-erected in their original location. So far, the request has been refused.

Our Psalmist, this morning, laments the fact that he and his companions also find themselves 'in a strange land'. Cut off from Jerusalem, following its destruction by the Chaldeans, he weeps, as he remembers Zion and reflects upon all it meant to him and his people. God had acted in judgement; exile may have been deserved; but the pain it brings is unremitting: 'How could we sing the Lord's song in a foreign land?' He prays fervently that he will never forget Jerusalem. By contrast, the writer to the Ephesians speaks powerfully of the undeserved grace of God – a God, rich in mercy, overflowing

* In the Anglican cycle the Old Testament reading for today is Numbers 21:4–9 and the Psalm is 107:1–9.

with generous love, who has 'made us alive together with Christ'. Just as Cyrus was God's instrument in enabling the return of the exiles to Jerusalem, so, by his death and resurrection, Jesus Christ, God's only-begotten Son, was to become the instrument of humanity's return to God. He came not to condemn, but to save.

The message of grace and salvation is no different today to what it was two thousand years ago. It is the message we are still called faithfully to proclaim in our churches, and our market-places, among our families and even in the 'strange lands' of exile where we may sometimes find ourselves to be. Those lands may be actual, as we are physically displaced into a new community or into a different culture, or they may be metaphorical, as we find ourselves in those situations where, although everything around may remain familiar, we feel we no longer belong, because we think or believe differently to those around us. We are not alone: for many of those around us feel in exile too. At such times, God invites us, like the Psalmist, never to forget – to recall that our relationship with God is our 'highest joy', and to ponder the truth that 'we are what he has made us to be' – God's work of art. We have been fashioned with extreme carefulness, created out of love, restored to our rightful place in Christ Jesus – made all that he intended us to be – because he loved us so much that he gave us his Son. It is a message we need to hear afresh for ourselves, and a truth we are called to share with all those who still weep by their River of Babylon and long to 'come home'.

You have made us for yourself, and our hearts are restless until they find their rest in you.[34]

FOURTH SUNDAY OF LENT (YEAR C)*

Homecoming

Joshua 5:9–12
Psalm 34
2 Corinthians 5:16–21
Luke 15:1–3, 11b–32

The Arrivals Lounge at an international airport is a fascinating venue for a bit of 'people-spotting'. There are those who are there simply to pick up a visiting businessperson and ferry them to a meeting or to their hotel. There are the long lost acquaintances who wonder whether they will recognise an old college friend when they see one. There are family members or friends who are there to collect grandma and granddad, who have just returned from their winter break in the Mediterranean. Then there are the spouses and lovers, who have ticked the days off the calendar and yearned for this moment – for their lover's return – excited and relieved that the day has at last come.

Homecoming is a common thread in today's readings. Joshua and the recalcitrant people of Israel have finally arrived in their Promised Land; they pitch camp at Gilgal and celebrate the Passover, shedding, at last, the disgrace of their captivity in Egypt. The past is behind them; they can make a new start. Today's Gospel reading is probably the most well-known homecoming in the whole of the New Testament. The prodigal returns after weeks of debauchery and poverty to find a warmth of welcome from his father he could never have

* In the Anglican cycle the Psalm for today is Psalm 32.

imagined: the best robe, a ring for his finger, sandals for his feet, a fatted calf and a celebration meal. There is no doubt about the joy and anticipation surrounding *this* homecoming. But 'homecoming' is different to 'arriving' – as the variety of people in an international airport illustrates. Some are just on business: they don't know anybody and they are simply met and delivered by a member of the company. For others, there is much more excitement and joy: it is, in a very real sense, a homecoming – such as with the grandparents, and the lover or spouse. So homecoming is not simply about coming back to a place you have left. Homecoming is about being in the right relationship with the people who matter, wherever you might be in terms of physical place or space. Homecoming is about return to where you belong; in the spiritual sense, therefore, it is about coming back to God.

Most people who read this book will know something of what I am talking about. You will have 'come home' time and time again, and known the Father's embrace and joy. You will know what it is to turn back, to repent and to receive the gracious forgiveness and mercy of God. Yet there are many in our world who know nothing of this homecoming, who continue to wander in a wilderness, or fritter their lives away in a foreign land, without purpose or hope. To us, his disciples and ministers, God speaks through St Paul, and says, '[God] has given us the ministry of reconciliation ... We are ambassadors for Christ, since God is making his appeal through us.' Isn't it time we went out to meet them?

The mystery indeed is that God in her (sic) infinite compassion has linked herself for eternity with the life of her children. She has freely chosen to become dependent on her creatures, whom she has gifted with freedom. This choice causes her grief when they leave; this choice brings her gladness when they return. But her joy will not be complete until all who have received life from her have returned home and gather together around the table prepared for them.[35]

MONDAY IN WEEK 4

Joy comes with the morning

Isaiah 65:17–21
Psalm 30:1–5, 8, 11–end
John 4:43–end

A glance at the newspaper over breakfast is not normally calculated to raise a smile; listening to the *Today* programme on Radio 4 is more likely to create a sense of irritation or despair than a warm 'inner glow'. Terrorist attacks in the Middle East, another coup in West Africa, a rise in the number of AIDS cases in Europe ... And when you read the Church press, you could sometimes be excused for thinking that God has 'gone on holiday' and all his people are interested in is the maintenance of the organisation. Money is short; people are weary; theological bickering is rife; and good news is hard to find. A caricature, perhaps, but, so often, even the Church seems to present its cup as 'half empty' rather than 'half full'.

What a different sense permeates today's readings! The Psalmist writes: 'I will extol you, O Lord, for you have drawn me up ... Sing praises to the Lord ... give thanks to his holy name.' To Israel, God says: 'Be glad and rejoice forever ... for I am about to create Jerusalem as a joy and its people as a delight.' And the royal official, whose son is at death's door, hearing Jesus' promise that his son will live, 'believed the word that Jesus spoke to him and started on his way.' God's promise of healing, of a renewed future – for individuals and communities – draws out a response of faith and hope and joy.

The season of Lent is – rightly – a period in the Church's year for sober reflection; but sober reflection is not the same as despondency. We acknowledge our sinfulness – but only in the light of God's promised forgiveness. We acknowledge our weakness – but only in the light of God's promised strengthening. We acknowledge our shortcomings – but only in the light of the God who promises to 'draw us up' and 'turn our mourning into dancing'. Ours is a faith that is rooted in what God has done in Christ, and that gives us hope – whatever the trials and suffering we, or our world, have to face. Our cup is not just 'half full' (as opposed to 'half empty'). No, because of Christ's saving death and resurrection, it is positively overflowing!

None of this is to detract from the reality we see round about us; but it is to view it with a different perspective. Happiness can be superficial. Joy is *never* so – and it is joy that is to characterise our living as disciples. Sometimes it seems like a rare gift; something strangely unattainable. Perhaps, rather, it is something the Christian community should pray for especially. *Every* morning.

Imperturbable, mighty,
ruinous and compelling,
Sorrow and Joy
– summoned or all unsought for –
processionally enter.
Those they encounter
they transfigure, investing them
with strange gravity
and a spirit of worship.[36]

TUESDAY IN WEEK 4

A powerful force

Ezekiel 47:1–9, 12
Psalm 46:1–9
John 5:1–3, 5–16

On 26 December 2004, 'the mountains shook in the heart of the sea' and a tsunami caused devastation to countless communities in nations around the Indian Ocean: hundreds of thousands dead, millions homeless, miles and miles of coastland flattened. It was a natural disaster on an unprecedented scale, eliciting an unprecedented humanitarian response. And the question it left so many asking was 'Where was God in it all?' It was, of course, a question that supplied its own answer. For God was, indeed, in the middle of it all – in the suffering of injury and bereavement, in the overflowing of human compassion and practical aid that followed, and in the steady rebuilding of lives and communities that have lived through the disaster to greet a new dawn. Water had caused devastation, but it was also a means to new life.

Water – its power to destroy and give life – is a common theme in today's readings. Ezekiel's vision of the water flowing from the sanctuary of God conveys both its force and its fertility – 'a river that could not be crossed' yet one lined by 'a great many trees' giving food to eat and leaves for healing. In today's Gospel, the healing theme continues as the 'stirring of the waters' of Bethzatha becomes the cue for Jesus to heal the paralytic of thirty-eight years – despite the latter's apparent disinclination to be restored to health. Water is a powerful force, an agent for both good and ill, and God is at work through it.

'Being an agent for God' is part of what it means to be a disciple, and what is true of every disciple is especially true for those who lead. For the public figure who is the minister, the priest or the chaplain, is often the one who, in the midst of disaster – personal or corporate – is asked, 'Where is God in it all?' and whose response can carry a weight beyond words. To be called to exercise such an authority, to be, potentially, a powerful force for good or ill, can leave us feeling very exposed, and yet, by God's grace, it can also be the very means through which healing comes. Jesus uses his authority to challenge and to heal, to confront and to cure – even when people seem hardly to care about the outcome. His willingness to be exposed to the criticism and judgement of others – even to seek it out as he does in today's Gospel reading – becomes the means by which many are touched by God. Perhaps those of us who, in our ministries, sometimes have to face the tidal waves of disaster head on, may be encouraged to respond with trust in the God who brings life and fruit and healing, and who is ever-present by his Spirit as our refuge and strength.

'You will never be overcome.' God wants us to pay attention to these words, so as to trust him always with strong confidence, through thick and thin. For he loves us, and delights in us; so he wills that we should love and delight in him in return, and trust him with all our strength. So all will be well.[37]

WEDNESDAY IN WEEK 4

Abandonment

Isaiah 49:8–15
Psalm 145:8–18
John 5:17–30

To be a disciple can be a lonely calling. To be the minister or priest of a Christian community can sometimes leave one feeling desolate. Dennis knew something of that sense of isolation. He'd been working in the villages for six years. Things had gone well – some of the time; but recently he'd begun to have a sense that no one cared any more. The bishop hadn't been for four years; his colleagues thought he was odd; and his people took him for granted. Nobody said anything positive any more: they just complained about trivial things and expected him to think of everything and to *do* it as well. He felt fed up, forgotten and alone. And, some days, God seemed to have abandoned him too ...

Today's readings paint a very different picture. The Psalmist proclaims God's faithfulness, steadfast love and compassion: God is good to all – one upon whom the whole of creation may *and must* depend. He is a listening, generous God – one who opens his hand, 'satisfying the desire of every living thing'. God is interested; more than that, God 'upholds all who are falling and raises up all who are bowed down.' The prophet Isaiah delivers a similar message: God has not abandoned his people, but promises comfort and compassion and restoration and hope. A nursing mother might forget her child, but God will never forget his chosen.

When we think of abandonment, we tend to think of it in

a purely negative sense: an abandoned vehicle, an abandoned village, an abandoned child. To be (or to feel) abandoned is not a good thing. But abandonment can also be positive – not in the passive sense in which we most usually use it, but in the *active* sense of the verb. It's as if we say, 'I abandon myself, my concerns, my situation to the care and protection of someone else. I can do nothing. In short, I abandon myself and all that I am to God.' It is an active *choice*, a 'letting go' to God. In today's Gospel, Jesus demonstrates this utter dependence upon the Father as he says, 'I can do nothing on my own'. On the cross, he demonstrates abandonment in *both* its forms as he cries out, in lonely agony, 'My God! Why have you forsaken me?' and then is able to affirm with confidence, 'Into your hands I commend my spirit.'

Loneliness and isolation is a common experience of discipleship and ministry. To ask for grace to discover abandonment in the *positive* sense of that word is to ask to be more like the Jesus of the cross – and *that* is a prayer of dependence we may seek to pray daily.

Abandonment is receiving all things the way one receives a gift:
With opened hands, an opened heart.
Abandonment to God is the climactic point in any man's [sic] life ...
Abandonment is more than commitment. It is deeper.
It is not doing anything for God, but being done by God.[38]

THURSDAY IN WEEK 4

Approved?

Exodus 32:7–14
Psalm 106:19–23
John 5:31–47

References for jobs, performance targets, job appraisal, departmental review: our world is increasingly drawn to measure the worth of its inhabitants by means of human approval, human testimony and human value. If you want to get on in the world, then you need to ensure that others recognise your worth and measure it in some way: either by what you achieve in the workplace or demonstrate in the marketplace. Such a world creates an environment in which competition is rife and people become ever more dependent on the affirmation of others as a reason to keep trying. They feel loved not for who they are, but for what they can achieve – either for themselves or for their employer. Dog eats dog, and contentment vanishes.

Sadly, the Church can be all too similar. For all its benefits, the stranglehold of secular management theory on the Church's way of working means that – like so many of our fellow-disciples – those who lead the Church can become caught up into a pattern of appraisal and approval that breeds dependence on *human* testimony, rather than *God's* testimony. Ministry review (as it is sometimes known) can be a great benefit in helping leaders to reflect on their work and to be encouraged and valued by their peers and colleagues. Yet it brings in its wake the danger of falling into the trap of its secular counterpart: the need to prove one's effectiveness and to avoid any sense of incompetence, for fear it might damage one's 'career'.

Jesus has some firm things to say about human approval: in short, he doesn't need it, because he has his heavenly Father's approval, and it is manifest in the works he does on his Father's behalf. Jesus doesn't need others in order to know that he is loved, since he lives within the constant circle of his Father's love, by the Holy Spirit dwelling within him. The Jews to whom Jesus is speaking in our Gospel reading are looking for all sorts of ways to ensure that this rabbi is genuine – looking, if you like, for good references and tangible evidence of his ministry. He will not oblige, other than to tell them to read their Scriptures with insight and to believe what they see!

Those who follow Jesus Christ and who walk with others on the way, participate, with him, in the life of God by the Holy Spirit already dwelling within them. God testifies in Christ that he loves them. They need nothing more. They have all the approval they require. We all need affirmation and encouragement – they are gifts we can offer each other, both formally and informally – but they do not, and cannot, *create* a person's value before God and human beings; they simply *confirm* it. It is an important distinction to remember.

O my God, I believe not only in your infinite goodness which embraces the whole world, but also in that particular and wholly personal goodness which embraces me – poor creature that I am. And that is why, Lord, even when I see nothing, when I feel nothing, and when I understand nothing, I believe that all I am and all that comes to me is the work of your love.[39]

FRIDAY IN WEEK 4*

Courage, challenge and truth

Wisdom 2:1, 12–22
Psalm 34:15–end
John 7:1–2, 10, 25–30

It takes courage to speak out against the prevailing mores of the day; and yet those who do are often remembered with awe and respect, as history vindicates their willingness to be the prophetic voice to nation or institution or church. Names like Bishop George Bell, Dietrich Bonhoeffer and Desmond Tutu come to mind; Steve Biko, Oscar Romero and Janani Luwum, to name but a few. Little surprise, perhaps, that, of these, half met a violent and untimely death at the hands of those whose evil deeds they condemned. The truth is often hard to hear as well as hard to bear.

When God calls Jeremiah to go into the temple and to prophesy its destruction and the desolation of Jerusalem, the priests, the prophets and the people don't like it at all. They close in on Jeremiah and try, unsuccessfully, to persuade the officials to convict him so that he might be 'disposed of' and silenced forever. But it is not to be: Jeremiah persists in speaking out – confident in his commission from God, and prepared to go on saying the difficult things at the time and in the places that God directs. The similarities with Jesus' visit to Jerusalem at the Feast of Tabernacles are obvious. Here is another 'prophet', called by God to speak out – at the right time – and to challenge the people and their religious leaders

* In the Anglican cycle the Old Testament reading is Jeremiah 26:8–11.

to make a choice: is Jesus the Messiah or not? By claiming that he has come from God, Jesus puts them on the spot and forces them to discern the truth about who he really is.

Courage, challenge and truth are words that all disciples need to take seriously. Whether in the intimacy of conversation with another, or in the public exposure of speech or lecture or sermon, there are moments when all may be called to speak with the voice of the prophet, to utter the uncomfortable word, to impose the difficult choice. But, like Jeremiah and Jesus himself, we are called to be confident in our commission and to trust in God's timing. It may cost us our reputation; it has cost some their lives. It takes courage to challenge others; our natural inclination may be to run away and try to avoid it. Instead, we are invited to rest on the promise that 'The Lord redeems the life of his servants: none of those who take refuge in him will be condemned.'

[The Church's] supreme concern is not the victory of the national cause. It is a hard thing to say, but it is vital. Its supreme concern is the doing of the Will of God, whoever wins, and the declaring of the Mercy of God to all men (sic) and nations.[40]

SATURDAY IN WEEK 4

Head and heart

Jeremiah 11:18–20
Psalm 7:1–2, 8–11
John 7:40–52

As people were leaving the service, a woman stopped and said to the vicar: 'Thank you for the way you led us this morning; sometimes, it just sounds as if people are saying the words – but with you, I could tell you really meant it.' Leading worship is a regular part of a minister's task; but some days, it can seem like just another thing to be done in an already busy schedule. Fortunately (for both leader and congregation), the efficacy of the sacrament and the value of worship is not dependent upon the spiritual state of the person leading. Instead, it rests solely on the grace of God and the working of the Holy Spirit. Nevertheless, what the woman acknowledged that day, was a personal integrity in the vicar – an *integration*, if you like, of head, heart and action – that spoke openly (yet silently) of his *own* life of faith as well as that implicit in the words of the liturgy. She could tell that he believed what he said with both head and heart.

Today's readings prompt us to look at this link between head and heart. There is an endearing naivety that emerges through today's passage from Jeremiah: until God reveals it to him, the 'gentle lamb' is, it seems, oblivious to the fact that the people are trying to slaughter him! It's as if he's so tuned in spiritually, that his common sense has disappeared. By contrast, the Pharisees are so immersed in keeping the letter of the Law and interpreting the predictions of Scripture concerning the Messiah, that they fail to allow either his teaching or his person to penetrate the thick skin of their intellect and touch their hearts. The exception, it seems, is Nicodemus – the one who had met Jesus by night – and whose heart had been moved by the invitation to be 'born again of water and the Spirit'. What is clear from all of today's readings is that God tests both mind and heart; and we can hide nothing from him.

And so the *cantus firmus* of Lent goes on ... And we are invited to fall to our knees again, in penitence for our waywardness and in sorrow for our sinfulness. It is not that our intellect is harmful in itself; on the contrary, it is a God-given gift to be offered back and used to understand the Scriptures, to deepen faith and to stretch minds in search of God. But it can never be a substitute for faith, for that heart-response to the embrace of God that draws us deeper into the one who is Love. *That* is a gift, given through prayer and lives lived, daily, in the heart-knowledge of the God who knows us from the inside and longs for us to know him too.

By our reason we obtain fresh light on our concepts, but it is by faith that we respond to life ... Faith enables us to grasp life as a whole, moment by moment; by faith we rise above all that we see or understand or feel, and touch directly the living God, who cannot be attained by reason. There you have the difference between the erudition of a scholar and the life of a saint.[41]

FIFTH WEEK OF LENT

Take up thy cross, and follow Christ,
Nor think till death to lay it down;
For only he who bears the cross
May hope to wear the glorious crown.

FIFTH SUNDAY OF LENT (YEAR A)

Purveyors of hope

Ezekiel 37:1–14
Psalm 130
Romans 8:6–11
John 11:1–45

When my two sons were little, one of their favourite bedtime stories was *Funny Bones.* It was a story about a skeleton who, one day, had an accident and fell apart, but then found that he had been wrongly put back together; where there should have been a *femur* there was a *humerus*, and where there should have been a *tibia* there was a *fibula*. This amusing story (which was accompanied by the 'rattlings' of a delightfully scored cassette tape) told of Funny Bones' quest to get himself put back together again in the right way. He was only a skeleton, but he needed somebody to bring him back to life.

There is something comic about Ezekiel's vision of dry bones: and here is not just *one* dismembered skeleton, but a vast multitude of the whole house of Israel. The prophet's (slightly ridiculous) task is to prophesy to the bones and command them to come back together, to be clothed in sinews and flesh – ready to live again. Ezekiel does what the Lord commands, but he is only partially successful: there are bodies, but no life. The breath (or spirit) is not in them; and so he has to prophesy to the breath in order to bring the house of Israel back to life as well.

Today, we find ourselves two-thirds of the way through Lent. In the Anglican calendar, it is Passion Sunday; in the

Roman calendar, the Sunday of that name is another week away. Whatever its name, the lectionary narrative is beginning to draw us closer, nearer, further in, towards the poignant and painful recollection of the Passion of our Lord. Easter is only two weeks away and already we are confronted with matters of life and death. Ezekiel has a vision of bones brought back to life by the Spirit of God. St Paul speaks of the Spirit of God bringing life to the mortal bodies of those who are in Christ; and, in the Gospel for today, Jesus raises his friend, Lazarus, from death as a foretaste of what is to be fulfilled through his own death and resurrection. Here is no avoiding death: it is faced head on.

Those who have been filled with the Spirit of God already have life, and are called to be purveyors of hope to those who do not. Each in their own way, Ezekiel, Paul and Jesus obediently fulfilled that calling. In this season of Passiontide, our vocation as disciples is, indeed, to follow in the way of the cross, but also to be such purveyors of hope. We are not only to face death (ours and his), but to breathe hope and life into a world in mourning. 'O Israel, hope in the Lord! For with the Lord there is steadfast love, and with him is great power to redeem.'

Spirit of God on the waste and the darkness,
Hovering in power as creation began,
Drawing forth beauty from clay and from chaos,
Breathing God's life in the nostrils of man (sic).
Come and sow life in the waste of our being,
Pray in us – form us – as sons (sic) of the Son.
Open our hearts to yourself, mighty Spirit,
Bear us to life in the Three who are One.[42]

FIFTH SUNDAY OF LENT (YEAR B)

A matter of death and life

Jeremiah 31:31–34
Psalm 51:1–12
Hebrews 5:5–10
John 12:20–33

A group of ordinands were told at the beginning of their pre-ordination retreat that they were being ordained to die. It was a bit of a shock. The retreat conductor had given each of them a tiny grain of wheat to hold, and was leading a meditation on words from today's Gospel: 'Very truly, I tell you, unless a grain of wheat falls into the earth and dies, it remains just a single grain; but if it dies it bears much fruit.' The ordinands were asked to imagine themselves as that grain of wheat: small, hard, rough, apparently insignificant, with a hard, protective outer shell, but with huge potential when planted in the right soil. The problem was, the grain of wheat had to die in order for life to grow.

This pattern of death and resurrection, played out a million times in nature every day, is the pattern of so much Christian living. It is seen in the sacraments of baptism and Eucharist; it is seen in the pattern of repentance, forgiveness and reconciliation at the heart of so much pastoral ministry. Above all, it is seen in the ministry of Jesus Christ himself. Jesus knows that life will come only through his death: he has to allow the grain of his earthly life to die, so that by the Father's transforming and mighty power, others will know the fruit of his resurrection life. For Jesus, as for his disciples, it is a pattern of giving up in order to receive back; a pattern of losing in order to find and be found.

This is the pattern of discipleship he offers to all who want to serve him. Following Christ as servant means being willing to lose life in order to find it for eternity. It is not a 'pick 'n' mix' kind of following: 'I'll do that, but I can't do *that*.' No, it's all or nothing. For clergy, it is about being ordained into Christ's death so as to become ministers of his life to others. For all of us, it is an awesome demand. What is crucial, however, is to remember that it is *God* who gives the life, by the work of the Holy Spirit within us and among us. That was what was so different about the new covenant about which the prophet Jeremiah spoke. God says to his people, 'I will put my law within them, and I will write it on their hearts.' There is nothing they, or we, can do to make the hard grain of wheat that we are, spring into life without *him*. Life is sheer gift, the fruit of ministry sheer grace. And grains that are planted, watered, harvested, milled, baked and shared become – together – bread for the world.

That the tedium of giving in the risk of surrender
and the reaching out, naked, to a world that must wound,
may be kindled fresh, daily, to a blaze of compassion;
that the grain may fall, gladly, to burst in the ground
and the harvest abound.[43]

FIFTH SUNDAY OF LENT (YEAR C)*

Forward momentum

Isaiah 43:16–21
Psalm 126
Philippians 3:4b–14
John 8:1–11

During exam season, tensions run high. Those who sit public exams, in school, college or university, often emerge from the examination room and want to review everything they've just written: the post-mortem can be encouraging or discouraging depending upon whether the answers you came to were or were not the same as everybody else's! The trouble with exams, however, is that once they're over, there's no going back. You can't go back into the room and change what you've written. You can't do anything at all to change the grade you will be given. They can leave you feeling elated or dejected, but whether it's gone well or badly, the best advice is to look forward and press on.

Today, the season of Lent seems to take on a momentum of its own. Two weeks to go – and what has, until now, been a steady journey of reflection, seems to gather speed towards its inevitable denouement: the Passion of Holy Week and the celebration of Easter Day. So it is something of a surprise to find that the readings set for today are so full of joy. The clear message from Isaiah is 'Don't look back, look forward!': 'Do not remember the former things, or consider the things of old. I am about to do a new thing ...' Paul, in Philippians,

* In the Anglican cycle the Gospel reading is John 12:1–8.

exudes a similar forward momentum. The past is to be counted as mere rubbish: what matters is what lies ahead, and the goal of 'the prize of the heavenly call of God in Christ Jesus.' This is what he is straining for with every sinew of his being.

Looking forward and knowing your goal are important elements of the life of discipleship. So often we can be tempted to dwell on the past, to ruminate on things that have happened – for good or ill – and that we are powerless to change. Sometimes, of course, our dwelling on the past is because we are aware of our failings, our need for forgiveness, or our need to forgive; but often, we are simply worried or anxious or unwilling to let go and move on. It is in such circumstances that the Sacrament of Reconciliation can bring release and comfort: to minister it is a privilege not to be taken for granted; to receive it is to allow tears and weeping to be transformed into joy and deliverance.

But what about knowing the goal? Those who sit examinations usually have a particular end in view – qualifications for a job, getting into college or university or getting a degree. It is sometimes more difficult for disciples to keep their focus. Today's readings give us a chance to reflect on our own 'forward momentum': to examine whether there is anything holding us back that we may need to confess, and to set our eyes afresh on the prize of our heavenly calling. For the road we walk, we walk in the company of him who suffered and was raised and is now seated at the right hand of God. And he has made us his own.

In very wide circles, the practical loss of the habit of confessing to a priest – as a quite normal thing – has led to an almost complete loss of any sense of sin. It is not because confession is too easy, but because it is too difficult.[44]

MONDAY IN WEEK 5*

Condemned

Susanna 1–9, 15–17, 19–30, 33–62
Psalm 23
John 8:1–11

When Charles was accused of 'inappropriate behaviour' by one of his parishioners, there was very little he could do to defend himself: it was her word against his, and whom would the bishop believe? Whatever the outcome of the inquiry, his reputation would be forever tarnished, and the pastoral ministry of the parish stained with lingering questions about his motives and actions. He could protest his innocence, but would anybody ever accept his word? It was like 'walking through the darkest valley'. He felt powerless; and, in the end, only God would exonerate him at the Day of Judgement.

For Susanna and the woman caught in adultery in our Gospel, there is a similar sense of helplessness – at least until the intervention by the 'man of God'. Each has been tricked by men – men who either lust after their bodies or who are prepared to use them for their own ends, placing no value whatsoever on them as persons. They are pawns in a man's game and powerless to defend themselves. Yet what shines through is a strong sense that these two women are prepared to face whatever comes their way, confident in God himself. Susanna refuses to be led into sin, and trusts in the intimate knowledge and justice of God. The woman caught in

* In the Anglican cycle the Old Testament reading is Joshua 2:1–14.

adultery simply stands before Jesus, helpless and dependent upon the mercy and wisdom of the one who draws in the dust. She awaits the sting of the first stone: and it doesn't come.

Condemnation can afflict many who choose to follow Christ. Perhaps it is not surprising – for we are called to follow in the way of one who was, himself, unjustly condemned. For us, it can come in various ways and with varied degrees of severity; from a simple complaint about something that has been done, to an allegation of a criminal offence. In such situations, the media have a field day. Those in authority in the Church can be especially vulnerable to such accusations – true or false – and living with the consequences can be terrible.

One of the striking things about today's readings is that, in the midst of the horror, God is present: in the person of Daniel, in the person of Jesus and in the confidence of the Psalmist. It is noticeable that the table is prepared 'in the presence of my enemies' – a pre-echo, perhaps, of the Last Supper, where Judas dips his bread in the bowl and then rushes out into the night to do his worst? Those who condemn are brought to justice. Those who are condemned receive mercy. For, where there is condemnation – on whatever scale – *there is God*, who, in Christ carried everything that condemns and is condemned on aching shoulders to the cross, and there redeemed it, once and for all.

Are you not willing to suffer also for him? To endure the contradiction of sinners?[45]

TUESDAY IN WEEK 5

Thick as two short planks

Numbers 21:4–9
Psalm 102:1–3, 15–23
John 8:21–30

There is a well-known story (apocryphal or not) about the priest who arrived in his new parish and preached the same sermon, week in, week out. The churchwarden, who had begun to receive numerous complaints from parishioners, finally plucked up courage to ask the new incumbent why it was that he only ever preached one sermon. The classic answer that emerged was, 'When you start to act on what I am saying in *this* one, then I'll preach another!' The message, it seems, was simply not getting through.

One senses something of this irritation in today's Gospel reading. Jesus is teaching in the Temple precincts, explaining to the Pharisees (and anybody else who will listen) that he is the Messiah, sent by God the Father to bring salvation to the Jews and to all people. He tries and tries, but the message is simply not getting through and in the end, the frustrated Jesus exclaims, 'Why do I speak to you at all?' His audience are, it seems, as thick as two short planks! In the end, it is only his death on the cross, so poignantly resonant of the bronze serpent in the wilderness, that will make them realise who he really is, and how deep the Father's love. 'When you have lifted up the Son of Man, then you will realise that I am he.' The God who judges his people in their sinfulness, also provides the means to their salvation by the gift of his Son.

And that is where the phrase 'as thick as two short planks'

takes on a curiously profound double meaning. Our stumbling ignorance and blindness as disciples leads us to impatience, complaining, detours around the difficulties of life, misunderstandings of all sorts: we moan both *at* each other and *about* each other and so lose any sense of direction, purpose and focus. Like the people of Israel, we can find ourselves lost in a wilderness of sinfulness and unbelief. God 'inclines' towards us in love again and again; and yet the message simply doesn't get through. Like the priest in his new parish, God keeps on speaking the same message to his world and, like Moses, invites us, his disciples, to make that message of salvation and healing known. Perhaps, as we journey on towards the Passion, today may be a day for us to gaze afresh upon 'two short planks' raised up on a middle-eastern rubbish tip, and the suffering Son of God who even now longs to draw human beings into his embrace.

High and lifted up, I see Him on the eternal Calvary,
And two pierced hands are stretching east and west o'er land and sea.
On my knees I fall and worship that great Cross that shines above,
For the very God of Heaven is not Power, but Power of Love.[46]

WEDNESDAY IN WEEK 5

Liberating truth

Daniel 3:14–20, 24–25, 28
Canticle: Benedicite
John 8:31–42

The scan didn't lie. The cancer was rampant. The prognosis was grim. Yet Ruby was radiant, because now she knew. The waiting, the uncertainty was over; she knew she was going to die – and soon. Each time Stephen, her priest, visited this loyal and faithful parishioner in hospital, he was amazed at her inner strength; and he left having received far more than he felt he had given. For Ruby glowed with something 'other', something beyond herself. It was as if Jesus was there, right alongside her. All the anxiety and doubt of the preceding six months had drained away, and Ruby had found a freedom to live out her last days with a serenity and joy that nobody could have anticipated. In a very real sense, the truth had set her free.

In today's Gospel, Jesus tells those Pharisees who are on the brink of becoming disciples, that the same can be true for them. They know now. The uncertainty is over. The picture is absolutely clear. If they want to be his disciples, then they need to make his word their home. In other words, they are both to dwell *on*, and dwell *within*, the truth that he is the Messiah, the Son of God. They are not to deviate from that truth and fall back into a dependency on their inheritance as Abraham's children. Rather, they are to rely on the inheritance won for them by the Son of God himself. Any other foundation, any other framework of understanding will fail:

and they will remain as slaves to sin. Shadrach, Meschach and Abednego discovered something similar several hundred years earlier: although they were captive in an alien land, and subject to the despotic whims of its king, in the end it was the truth – and their utter loyalty to it – that set them free. They could follow the crowd into idolatry and avoid conflict and almost certain death, or they could stand up for what was true and put their trust in God. Like Ruby, what people saw in the midst of the inferno was God, right alongside them.

The challenge of today's Gospel is twofold. Firstly, it is to become those who make the word of God our home, so that the truth of God's love and loyalty towards us seeps ever deeper in, and we know ourselves to be his children. Secondly, it is to be those who *liberate truth* among those we serve, so that both they, and we, may be radiant with the serenity and joy of Christ himself. Ruby had discovered both. Yet, so many others are captive to the shadows of self-deception, past hurts, unresolved conflict and broken relationships. For disciples, surely, 'liberating truth' is both something to rejoice in and a task to undertake. For the truth sets us – and others – free.

A Christian has nothing to fear but the truth. For it alone could show that his movement is not of God ... But he also has nothing to fear in the truth. For to him the truth is Christ.[47]

THURSDAY IN WEEK 5

Sticks and stones

Genesis 17:3–9
Psalm 105:4–9
John 8:51–end

School playgrounds are not always the most peaceful of environments. In fact they can be decidedly unpleasant: a hotbed of petty squabbles and spiteful exchanges. One of the 'tools' I learnt as a young child, and which was supposed to fend off unwarranted unkindness, was the little rhyme: 'Sticks and stones may break my bones, but words can never hurt me.' It was, of course, untrue. Words *did* hurt. In fact, they penetrated deeply, and pretend as I might that all was well, there were many occasions when I escaped to the girls' toilets to have a good old cry on my own, or in the company of one of my 'best friends'.

Sticks and stones ... It is ironic (and, perhaps, deliberate) that John chapter 8 begins with a woman in hiding, under threat of stoning and ends with a man, also under threat of stoning, who goes into hiding. In both scenes, disturbing words have been exchanged. In the first, as we saw a few days ago, the Pharisees accuse the woman taken in adultery, and Jesus invites them to ponder their own innocence. In the second, Jesus claims he is greater than Abraham and the prophets – 'Before Abraham was, I am' – and the enraged religious leaders can do nothing but condemn him for blasphemy and pick up stones to launch at him. Little surprise he leaves the Temple precincts and goes into hiding!

Children in playgrounds, domestic strife, friction between

colleagues, political argument, dissension in the Church: all contexts where words can both disturb and destroy. Now, disturbance is sometimes necessary and can be very creative: there is, for example, truth in the old adage that a good sermon will 'disturb the comfortable and comfort the disturbed'. There *are* occasions when we are called to disturb – to challenge presuppositions and question assumptions – and to do so can be disturbing for *us* too. People may feel threatened, reactions may be strong, and our message may appear to be in complete contradiction to all they hold dear. In the process, we make ourselves vulnerable – just like Jesus himself. Indeed, in some parts of the world, disciples are – quite literally – stoned for witnessing to their faith in an alien environment. But words can equally be used to destroy – to make the hearers vulnerable, to cause hurt and upset in a way that is vindictive and cruel rather than helpful and edifying. Such disturbing words are not to be found on the lips of disciples, as the Letter of James and Jesus himself make plain.

So what about you? Have you, knowingly, used words to hurt and destroy? Are you guilty of 'throwing stones' at other people? Or is God asking you to be a disturber? And are you prepared for the 'sticks and stones' that may follow?

The other gods were strong, but Thou wast weak;
They rode, but thou didst stagger to a throne.
But to our wounds, only God's wounds can speak,
And not a god has wounds, but Thou alone.[48]

FRIDAY IN WEEK 5

Under pressure

Jeremiah 20:10–13
Psalm 18:1–6
John 10:31–end

Only a few days to go, and the demands of preparing for Holy Week are upon us. Are the palm crosses ready? Has the Paschal candle arrived? And how many sermons, talks, anthems and intercessions are there yet to prepare? To say nothing of the normal run of pastoral and practical demands ... For everyone – lay and ordained alike – it is a pressured time of year.

Pressure is evident in each of our readings for today. Jesus is still doing verbal battle with the Pharisees: they openly accuse him of blasphemy and he steadfastly lays claim to his unique relationship with the Father. Jeremiah has become so unpopular that even his close friends have turned on him and are trying to trip him up and wreak their revenge. The Psalmist is surrounded by the threat of impending death, with enemies on every side. Commitment is strong; but the pressure is on. Jesus, we read, eludes arrest and escapes across the Jordan to continue his ministry in the place where John used to baptise. Jeremiah and the Psalmist both cry out to God for help, calling upon his protection and mercy and even for retribution. For God is a rock, a fortress, a deliverer, a refuge, a shield, a horn of salvation and a stronghold – strong images that can bring comfort and a sense of security to those who are weighed down with the stresses of life and ministry. Warrior and prophet alike cry out to the Lord in their distress and, we read, 'my cry to him reached his ears'.

Passages like these are a wonderful aid and support to those who are under pressure – for pressure there will certainly be for those who follow Jesus Christ; and it isn't always possible to avoid it, or escape to a safer place. Whether caused by demanding or difficult people, a mountain of administration, a tricky pastoral situation or the sheer busyness of Church life, we too can feel that 'terror is all around' and that people are out to make us stumble and fall. But there are two further things that, perhaps, remain to be said. Firstly, that the cries for deliverance are matched by shouts of praise. Much of the remainder of the Psalm describes the ways in which God has saved and protected his servants, but throughout, the glory is directed to God himself and not to the human victors. Even the doleful Jeremiah offers a 'Sing to the Lord; praise the Lord!' in the midst of his moaning! But there is one last reflection on today's Psalm that might so easily be missed – and that is to note the words with which the Psalm begins: 'I love you, O Lord, my strength.' Maybe those should be the first words on our lips when the pressure is really on?

Do we realise sufficiently fully that Christ never obliges anyone to love him? But he, the Living One, is there, poor and unknown, beside each person. He is there, even in the most difficult events, when our life is at its most vulnerable. His love is a presence, not for a fleeting moment but for ever. This is eternity's love, and it opens up for us a way of becoming that lies beyond ourselves.[49]

SATURDAY IN WEEK 5*

The only way out is through

Ezekiel 37:21–end
Jeremiah 31:10–13
John 11:45–end

I've never been white-water rafting. Those who have (and who enjoy that sort of thing) tell me that it is an exhilarating, thrilling and breathtaking experience. I'll take their word for it! The image of somebody climbing into a flimsy craft at the top of a steep fall of rapids is, nonetheless, a powerful one. Once the shore has been left and the current takes over, there is only one direction to go in. No giving up, no pulling in for a break, no escape: the only way out is through. But the joy and satisfaction written across the faces of those who relish this sort of extreme sport is absolutely clear: they wouldn't miss it for the world.

Today, on the eve of Holy Week, one has a similar sense of inevitability. A crossroads has been reached as we read, 'So from that day on they planned to put him to death.' Prompted by the divinely inspired prophecy of Caiaphas, the Pharisees resolve that the death of this one man is preferable to the destruction of a nation and its temple. Jesus is to be the scapegoat that will prevent Rome from overpowering and destroying the Jews completely. Yet this sombre prediction from today's Gospel is more than tempered by the overwhelming picture of hope that permeates both Jeremiah's

* In the Anglican cycle Psalm 121 may be read in place of Jeremiah 31:10–13.

and Ezekiel's words. There, God's promise for the future is announced: mourning will be turned to dancing; every grief will be consoled. Moreover, God's people will be gathered in – one flock with one shepherd – they will stream to Mount Zion, the covenant will be renewed and God will dwell among his people forever. It is a picture of restoration, of hope and unity and blessing.

Standing on the brink of Holy Week, it is all too easy to lose the sense of tension. On the one hand we risk being drawn into the story of the Passion as if it were a journey into a hopeless abyss. On the other, we can avoid truly identifying with our Lord, and walking in the way of the cross, because we know and believe the truth of resurrection. We need both: Good Friday and Easter Day. And that is where white-water rafting comes in. Once the Pharisees had made their decision to kill Jesus, it was only a matter of time: the die had been cast – the boat had been pushed away from the shore, and for Jesus, 'the only way out was through'. As we, ourselves, go into Holy Week, let us pray for grace to live with the tension – both the suffering and joy, the danger and the delight – and to recognise afresh what it cost him. For Jesus was to die 'not for the nation only, but to gather into one the dispersed children of God' – whoever they are and wherever they are from. And in the profoundest sense possible, he wouldn't have missed it – *for the world.*

Let us run with perseverance the race that is set before us, looking to Jesus, the pioneer and perfecter of our faith, who for the sake of the joy that was set before him endured the cross, disregarding its shame, and has taken his seat at the right hand of the throne of God.[50]

PASSION SUNDAY (PALM SUNDAY) AND HOLY WEEK

To thee, great Lord, the One in Three,
All praise for evermore ascend;
O grant us in our home to see
The heavenly life that knows no end.

PASSION SUNDAY (PALM SUNDAY)
(YEARS A, B AND C)

Celebrate!

Isaiah 50:4–7
Psalm 24
Philippians 2:5–11
A – Matthew 21:1–11
B – Mark 11:1–10 or John 12:12–16
C – Luke 19:28–40

Ask a novice policeman what has been his most frightening experience in the force so far, and there's a good chance he'll say something about crowd control. There's something about large groups of people that can be quite unnerving; football matches, pop concerts, student demonstrations come to mind, as feelings run high and emotions are released that any individual might be reticent to express. Crowds can be dangerous and hostile – a power to be reckoned with. But there is another dimension to a crowd that is, surely, less sinister: for crowds can also be 'permission-giving' in a positive and creative way. Think of the huge role crowds played in the late 1980s in the USSR, in Eastern Europe, in China and in South Africa: it is easier to say things and do things as one of the many rather than one of the few. Crowds can be 'safe' places, where you can express what's inside without being exposed; where you can influence what's going on without being labelled as a troublemaker or protagonist. Moreover, crowds reflect our human need for companionship, for community, for identification, for mutual understanding.

Crowds play a significant role in our Gospel reading today.

Faithful Jews from all around throng towards the holy city for the great festival of Passover. The atmosphere is expectant; the authorities are on their guard; and Jesus makes his entrance. No trumpets or chariots. No vanguard of zealots. No announcement of deliverance. Just a humble man on a donkey, walking with his friends. It was not something calculated to make an impression. Yet the crowd goes wild with excitement and celebration and joy: 'Hosanna to the Son of David!' It is a rapturous welcome. The authorities may have been perturbed, but the people were, at last, able to express their passion for this man who had come to save them.

This crowd was, of course, fickle. Within days, celebration had turned into condemnation, joy into judgement. And yet here, joy, expectation, enthusiasm and excitement overflow. The Saviour comes and the city rejoices. What about us? Will our corporate celebrations today reflect this joy? Will we celebrate with abandon, or will we temper our enthusiasm about the Saviour King, and restrain our excitement until next week? God has given us the capacity to celebrate. So, will we?

It was but now they gathered blooming May,
And of his arms disrobed the branching tree,
To strew with boughs and blossoms all thy way,
And now, the branchless trunk a cross for thee,
And May, dismayed, thy coronet must be:
It was but now they were so kind to throw
Their own best garments where thy feet should go,
And now, thyself they strip, and bleeding wounds they show.[51]

MONDAY IN HOLY WEEK*

Close friends

Isaiah 42:1–9
Psalm 27:1–3, 13–14
John 12:1–11

Christian ministry can be a lonely business. Not that there is usually any shortage of people around. Far from it! The demands of the populace can sometimes seem relentless. Perhaps it is more that there is a shortage of those one can call close friends; those who are there for you; those you can rely on; those with whom you can be yourself – away from the expectations of role and responsibility. Friends can be close in different ways, and sometimes we need to be careful about managing our relationships so that others are not hurt or threatened by them. Yet friends are extraordinarily important, and nurturing friendship is an oft-overlooked necessity.

In John's narrative, we move back in time to the evening before Palm Sunday. Jesus has taken refuge at the home of Mary, Martha and Lazarus in Bethany: he's feeling exposed and he needs his friends. Judas is there, as (probably) are the other apostles, and they are having dinner. Martha serves. Here she is in her characteristic sort of role, waiting on her guests, looking after their needs: close, but in a functional sort of way. Lazarus is at table with him, relishing the chance to be alive and enjoying Jesus' company: close, in a friendly sort of way. Judas is present too: looking on, questioning and

* In the Anglican cycle the Psalm is 36:5–11 and the Epistle is Hebrews 9:11–15.

condemning the actions of others: close, but in a 'distant' sort of way. And Mary? Yes, she too is in her characteristic place – kneeling at his feet, anointing them with costly ointment and drying them with her hair: close, and in an intimate sort of way. Four close friends – but all different.

Today's Gospel may prompt us to think about friendship at two different levels. What do we value most about our friends? What are their different strengths and weaknesses? How often do we take time to thank God for them and to thank *them* for who they are? But there's a deeper level ... Today's Gospel opens up the whole question of how *we* relate to Jesus. How close are we willing to become? Are we like Martha: close, but in a functional sort of way? Are we like Lazarus: close, and in a friendly sort of way? Are we like Judas: close, but in a 'distant' sort of way? Or are we like Mary: so passionate about our Lord that we are willing to kneel at his feet and weep and kiss and bathe him with the ointment of our love? For, surely, *this* is what he longs for.

Pray a lot: when we love, we want to talk endlessly to the being we love, or at least look at him endlessly: this is what prayer is, familiar converse with our Beloved: we look at him, we tell him we love him, we rejoice at being at his feet, we tell him that this is where we want to live and die.[52]

TUESDAY IN HOLY WEEK*

Lean on me

Isaiah 49:1–7
Psalm 71:1–17
John 13:21–33

When a new-born baby is delivered by the midwife, the first thing she does is lay the child on the mother's breast; warmth on warmth, flesh against flesh. The human need for touch and companionship is writ large in this simple act of being born, and held and loved. It is a crucial moment. As the child grows, there is a natural (and proper) growing apart, a growth made possible and safe by the parent's continuing love and support – by an implicit, reassuring 'You can depend on me,' at every stage. So, gradually, the separation that began with the severing of the umbilical cord finds its out-working in a healthy autonomy as child grows to adult and dependency gives way to responsibility.

Separation and dependency are key elements in today's Gospel reading. Jesus is preparing his closest followers for his going away: the final denouement is beginning. 'Little children, I am with you only a little longer ... Where I am going you cannot come.' Three years of working, living and ministering together is about to come to a sudden and violent end: the disciples will desert him and Jesus will walk the road to Golgotha alone. Judas has already left. Peter boasts of his

* In the Anglican cycle, the Epistle is 1 Corinthians 1:18–31 and the Gospel is John 12:20–36. For this latter, see reflection for The Fifth Sunday of Lent (Year B).

loyalty to his Lord, 'Lord, I will lay down my life for you,' and hears the shocking foretelling that, indeed, he *will* lay down his life in due time, but that he will also deny Jesus three times before the next sunrise. Tension is high, emotions near the surface, anxiety acute. By contrast, John leans, still, on Jesus' breast.

Each of us knows something of separation and dependency: it is part of what it is to be human. Whether it is separation from family or friends whom we love, from the people who have shaped us or from the places that have been special for us, there can be a longing for connection, for being together again, for a re-membering of the broken fragments of our lives. We need one another; and however adult or grown up we may be, there is always the child within than longs to rest again – just for a moment – on his mother's breast. We can tell ourselves (and others will tell us too) that we are strong, reliable, dependable and safe – and for most of us that is true, most of the time. In this Holy Week, perhaps it is sobering to reflect that, as disciples, we will sometimes be like Judas, sometimes like Peter, sometimes like John. For we too have the capacity to condemn, to betray, to boast, to deny. Yet we also have the capacity *and the need*, like a newborn child, to lean into the embrace of our Lord, and echo the Psalmist's words, 'Upon you I have leaned from my birth; it was you who took me from my mother's womb. My praise is continually of you.' But we have to allow ourselves to lean.

The Beloved Disciple is the type of complete discipleship. As the Son is in the bosom of the Father (i, 18) so the disciple is in the bosom of the Incarnate Son.[53]

WEDNESDAY IN HOLY WEEK*

Failure

Isaiah 50:4–9
Psalm 69:7–9, 20–21, 30, 32–33
Matthew 26:14–25

When I failed to pass my driving test at the first attempt, it was only the second time I had consciously failed at anything (the first was not getting into my first choice of University!). I found failure hard, and if I'm honest, I still do; but I suspect I'm not alone. In fact, I suspect most people struggle with failure and prefer to hide it or at least forget about it if they possibly can. Nigel was an Anglican priest, and when his marriage fell apart, he thought his ministry would too. For a while, it did, and he went back to work in broadcasting, where he quickly rose to be a producer. After a while, however, he followed his heart back into full-time ministry: and his ministry was never the same again. Not because he was no longer any good at it; on the contrary! Rather, his own experience of failure and the awareness of human frailty that came with it, made him a much better pastor – a much better priest. God used his apparent failure for the benefit of others.

We find ourselves, today, in the upper room. It is night. And it is the night before Jesus died. The scene is an intimate one: the disciples are gathered to celebrate the Passover meal. Jesus looks worried and disturbed. He says, 'Truly, I tell you,

* In the Anglican cycle, the Psalm is 70, the Epistle is Hebrews 12:1–3 and the Gospel is John 13:21–32. For this latter, see the reflection for Tuesday in Holy Week.

one of you will betray me.' A shiver ripples around the room: 'Surely not I, Lord?' And, as the others look on, Judas dips the bread in his hand into the bowl and finds himself cast in the role of betrayer – the one who will sell his Lord for thirty pieces of silver, and sell his soul in the process.

There is a Judas in each of us: one who has the capacity to look on, to condemn and even to betray. We condemn others by our critical eye, our disparaging attitudes, our 'holier-than-thou' way of behaving. We condemn ourselves through our lack of self-worth, our introspective preoccupation, our inability to love the person God has made us. In so doing, we condemn with our lips and betray with our actions our Lord himself. In short, we fail. Yet Judas was not evil: he was human. There is a very real sense in which Judas served his Lord to the end. Indeed, one could argue that without him – without his condemnation and betrayal of Jesus – God's plan of salvation might not have been fulfilled. God needed Judas, and Judas' failure was part of God's redeeming purpose. Today's Gospel reminds us that through the grace of God, every failure can be redeemed and every human frailty can become a means to salvation in Jesus Christ. Perhaps, in a sense, it is but a small reflection of the apparent 'failure' of the cross itself – a death that leads to life.

Christ has gone down into the deepest places of our failure and claimed them as his own, and now there is no possible failure in our lives or our deaths that cannot be the place of meeting him and of greater openness to his work.[54]

THURSDAY IN HOLY WEEK (MAUNDY THURSDAY)

Unless I wash you

Exodus 12:1–14
Psalm 116:1–2, 12–19
1 Corinthians 11:23–26
John 13:1–15

The symbolic act of washing feet has become an integral part of the Maundy Thursday Eucharistic liturgy. It is right that it should. For it enables the whole community of disciples to focus on the self-giving of Christ – not merely as an example of service, but as the one who was, himself, 'poured out' for the sake of the world, and whose saving death is remembered each time the Eucharist is celebrated. For the humiliation of foot-washing prefigures the humiliation of the cross; Christ's laying down of his garments prefigures the laying down of his life; the cleansing of the disciples' feet prefigures the cleansing of all humankind from the death of sin.

The story has often (and rightly) been used to encourage disciples to serve one another. They, like their Lord, are to be willing to kneel before their brothers and sisters and get their hands dirty. They are to be willing to be soiled by the dust and dirt of other people's lives and by the mess and dirt of a world scarred by tension, injustice, poverty, confusion and conflict. For it is here, in the stinking water of humanity's sinfulness that our loving God has chosen to become involved, and invites us, his Church, to participate too.

But there is a dimension to foot-washing that can so easily be overlooked, and it's something that only really begins to register when you allow somebody to wash *your* feet. Traditionally, it is the clergy who *do* the foot-washing, and perhaps that is right; but it is, surely, *more* demanding, *more* profound for the clergy to allow others to wash *them*? For in doing so they may begin to perceive that it is Christ himself who kneels at their feet and serves them. Perhaps it is something that is hard to accept? For to have your feet washed is to make yourself powerless; it is a place of *being*, and a place of *receiving*. It may be a place of argument, resistance, confusion, incomprehension – or it may be a place of wonder, depth, release and cleansing. It is, in short, a picture of the place of prayer, where God gives and we receive, where God loves us and we surrender, where God's humility gives birth to our humility, where his service of us becomes the source and springboard of our service to others.

The question is, will you *let* him wash your feet?

Divine humility shows itself in rendering service. But man's (sic) humility does not begin with the giving of service; it begins with the readiness to receive it ... Our first thought must never be, 'What can I do for God?' The answer to that is, 'Nothing.' The first thought must always be, 'What would God do for me?'[55]

FRIDAY IN HOLY WEEK (GOOD FRIDAY)*

Into your hands

Isaiah 52:13 – 53:12
Psalm 31
Hebrews 4:14–16; 5:7–9
John 18:1 – 19:42

The hour has come. Jesus is given up into the hands of wicked men – interrogated, condemned, mocked and crucified between two thieves. The Passion narratives re-told, day by day, during this Holy Week, have led us to live again the journey from Palm Sunday to the cross, and to enter into the traumatic sequence of events that make up this climax of the Christian year. We have walked with Christ and recognised ourselves in the crowd, in his disciples, in his accusers and in those who are responsible for his death: the whole of humanity is represented here, and so are we.

The Gospel writers each give us their own slant on events, and although today's Gospel is from John, it is St Luke who places on Jesus' lips words from today's Psalm: 'Into your hands I commit my spirit.' It is a cultic phrase used by the Psalmist to express his confidence and trust in God. In the face of difficulty, he affirms God's covenant faithfulness towards him as he places himself, willingly, into God's hands. It is a trust for life – a trust in times of distress, and specifically, a trust in the face of death. It's like the young child who has climbed up too high on a wall or becomes nervous at the top of a playground slide. A parent holds out

* In the Anglican cycle the Psalm is 22.

their hands to catch them as they jump or begin the long descent, and experience tells them it's safe to let go – they will not fall. 'Into your hands ...'

But those same words on the lips of Jesus at the crucifixion take on a different and deeper meaning. What, for the Psalmist, had been a cry for deliverance *from* death, becomes, for Jesus, a cry of confidence in the Father's love *even as he dies.* It is not a cry of resignation, but a cry of assurance – a letting go into the Father's hands.

To learn to say, 'Into your hands' is to learn the grace of allowing God to hold us: for Jesus Christ it was a grace expressed from the depths of pain made manifest in the glory of his suffering on the cross. For us, it is a grace we so often reject, preferring the Psalmist's *partial* understanding and crying out to God in the face of death and distress. There is nothing wrong in crying out to God for help – far from it – but there is more to it than that. On this Good Friday, may we learn anew the grace of letting go, *into his hands*, with that same confidence in the Father's love and purpose for us, that our Lord revealed on a hill outside Jerusalem.

... The earth is full of masks and fetishes,
what is there here for me? are these like him?
Keep company with him and you will know:
no kin, no likeness to those empty eyes.
He is a stranger to them all, great Jesus.
What is there here for me? I know
What I have longed for. Him to hold
me always.[56]

SATURDAY IN HOLY WEEK (HOLY SATURDAY)

The longest of days*

Job 14:1–14
Psalm 31
1 Peter 4:1–8
John 19:38–42

I have always felt uncomfortable entering a parish church on Holy Saturday and finding half a dozen industrious and wonderfully gifted flower-arrangers working away at splendid pedestals, pulpit and font adornments and window decorations; not that I have any objections to flowers and flower-arrangers – far from it. It is simply that it somehow feels too soon. Only hours after the Passion and pain of Good Friday, I am confronted with the anticipation of Easter Day, and I feel strangely cheated of the twenty-four hours in between.

Jesus is dead. And buried. Joseph of Arimathea, a secret disciple, has served his Lord in death in a way he could never have openly served him in life. Together with Nicodemus – another secret disciple – he has lavishly tended the distended corpse with expensive myrrh and aloes and laid the body in his own tomb. Two men united in grief and pain. It is the Day of Preparation. There will be a day of waiting until Sabbath is over.

Holy Saturday is, perhaps, the most neglected day of the Christian year. Yet it is a day that has a particular message of

* George Steiner, *Real Presences*, University of Chicago Press, Chicago, 1989, pp. 231–2.

its own. It speaks powerfully to us of an in-between time, a day when (as for the disciples) the pain and anguish of Good Friday resonates in our ears and hearts; a day when all seems to be lost; a day of never-ending hopelessness. Yet, equally, for the Christian, who lives with the perspective of the resurrection of Easter Day, Holy Saturday becomes a day, not of dark despair but of hopeful anticipation.

In our own scarred lives as disciples, and in a world that knows the suffering of oppression, war, natural and human disaster; a world in which infants die and terrorists seem to triumph, to live consciously through Holy Saturday can remind us that both the pain of Good Friday and the resurrection of Easter Day are held within the purposes of God in Christ. Moreover, the Church is called to minister in this in-between time, on this 'longest of days', to acknowledge suffering and anticipate resurrection, and so become the bearer both of pain and of hope in a waiting and wounded world. For many, Holy Saturday is a non-event. May it become for us today, a day to live with the anguish and the hope and the waiting of the in-between time, knowing that all things will be restored in and through the risen Christ.

Perhaps the flower-arrangers have got it right after all ...

It is in the very world of sickness, death and sin that joy and play take place, and Christ is Lord; and it is only in the context of injustice, negativity, and despair that we dare to speak of hope.[57]

EASTER DAY (YEARS A, B AND C)*

This is the day

Acts 10:34–43
Psalm 118:1–2, 14–24
Colossians 3:1–4
John 20:1–9

Six and a half weeks ago, we set out on a journey together. It is a journey that has, I trust, taken us deeper into the Scriptures, deeper into ourselves and deeper into God. Today, we arrive at a point that is always both an ending and a beginning. In the Church's year, it is the end of Holy Week and the beginning of Eastertide; the end of a season of penitence and introspection and the beginning of a season of rejoicing and hopeful witness to the world. And yet, for the disciple of Jesus Christ, it is the day (above all days) that gives meaning and value to every other: without the resurrection that we celebrate today, every day is hollow, every moment inconsequential. For in the resurrection of Jesus Christ from the dead, all humanity, all creation held within the bounds of time and space, has been brought again into right relationship with the creator of the universe. This is the day that the Lord has made – and it lasts for eternity.

Yet, it is a day upon which so much can be taken for granted. Even on the very first Easter Day, so many different assumptions are made. Mary Magdalene takes for granted that the body of Jesus has been stolen: she doesn't look into the tomb, but simply sees that the stone has been rolled away.

* This is a selection from the wide range of possible readings for today.

Peter takes for granted that he should go into the tomb, without hesitation, and almost (it seems) without respect. John takes for granted that Jesus is risen: 'Then the other disciple, who reached the tomb first, also went in, and he saw and believed.' Three different reactions within moments: one who assumed the worst; one who didn't even stop to think; one who dared to assume the best. And what is most striking about this third, of course, is that belief came *before* understanding.

It is very easy – particularly for those who have been disciples for many years – to take the resurrection message of Easter for granted. We know it too well, and somehow it is hard to read or hear the story with fresh eyes and ears. We cannot take ourselves back in time to join Mary or Peter or John in that garden two thousand years ago. We cannot pretend that the whole course of the Church's history has not taken place and that we are not inheritors of its ministry, tradition and truth; nor can we unravel the various threads – both joyful and painful – of our own Christian discipleship. What we *can* do this Eastertide, is to pray for a gracious re-freshening of the life and joy that was ours when we first believed (which may have been a long time before we began to *understand*), and for the continual grace and strength of God's Spirit, to help us go on living and proclaiming the good news of resurrection in his world.

You are walking now by faith, still on pilgrimage in a mortal body away from the Lord; but he to whom your steps are directed is himself the sure and certain way for you: Jesus Christ, who for our sake became human.[58]

THE COLLECT FOR EASTER DAY

Lord of all life and power,
who through the mighty resurrection of your Son
overcame the old order of sin and death
to make all things new in him:
grant that we, being dead to sin
and alive to you in Jesus Christ,
may reign with him in glory;
to whom with you and the Holy Spirit
be praise and honour, glory and might,
now and in all eternity.
Amen.

APPENDIX: SECOND SUNDAY OF LENT (ANGLICAN LECTIONARY YEAR A)

Only believe

Genesis 12:1–4a
Psalm 121
Romans 4:1–5, 13–17
John 3:1–17

I can well remember sitting late into the night in a student bedroom discussing the finer points of Christian apologetics – trying to persuade a group of my peers that following Jesus was really the only sensible way to live. Yet, for all my youthful zeal, they remained unconvinced. Then there were those other occasions when my fellow Christian Union members and I would share our anguish over the ways in which our lives didn't seem to match up to God's standards: we were sinful in 'thought, word and deed' and, hard as we might try, we never felt we had done enough in our Christian discipleship. Self-accusingly, we would mull over our faults and descend into a communal mire of despond. Shocking. Simple. But true.

When Nicodemus came to Jesus by night, he was determined to find out more about this Galilean rabbi. A man of good repute, a leading intellectual and teacher as well as a faithful keeper of the law of Moses, Jesus talks with him, taking his understanding deeper as they discuss the meaning of 'new birth' and the 'wind blowing where it will'. But the intellectual level is not enough. Instead, Jesus cuts through the layers of philosophy and argument to faith as God's *gift*. 'God so loved the world that he gave ...' says the Gospel reading: the challenge is to *believe*. We see something of this shocking simplicity of faith in the call of Abram and Paul's reflections on him: Abraham's righteousness – and God's blessing of him and all nations – depended not on anything he had *done*, but solely on God's grace and Abraham's obedient faith, a faith which was itself a gift from God. The way into the kingdom says Jesus (and says Paul), is neither by argument nor by effort: it's a case of 'only believe'. Shocking. Simple. But true.

Sometimes, it seems, ministers and disciples alike forget that what was true for Nicodemus and for Abraham is true for them also. Preaching the Gospel and serving the poor are, indeed, cornerstones of Christian living. Whether from the pulpit or the kitchen sink; whether in relief work in the Sudan or with the needy in our own back yard, every disciple has a duty to proclaim the good news in word and action. But 'The wind blows where it chooses.' We can pray for people to come to know God in Christ. We can give them a good intellectual case for choosing Christianity. We can demonstrate God's love for them through our pastoral care and community action: but we cannot make faith happen either for ourselves or for those we love and serve. Faith is, and always will be, *God's* gift – never ours. What God asks of us in serving him is what he asked of the Pharisee and the patriarch: only believe. Shocking. Simple. But true.

Theology normally begins in prayer, continues in thought and ends in prayer.[59]

SECOND SUNDAY OF LENT (ANGLICAN LECTIONARY YEAR B)

Deny yourself?

Genesis 17:1–7, 15–16
Psalm 22:23–31
Romans 4:13–25
Mark 8:31–38

I am told that anybody can walk a tightrope, provided they don't look at their feet. I'll take their word for it ... However, the moment the focus shifts from what lies ahead, to the apparently ridiculous idea of balancing a human body on a rope that is only eight centimetres in diameter, then all is lost. A rather extreme example, perhaps, of the understandable anxiety that can beset anybody who is asked to do something particularly challenging or demanding: like giving a speech at a wedding breakfast; like singing the office in public for the first time; like being asked to comment on television about a local or national crisis. Most of us cope reasonably well with such challenges until the point when we lose sight of the challenge and its purpose, and start to focus on ourselves. It's then that things can get shaky.

When Peter rebuked Jesus for speaking of his coming suffering, death and resurrection, it is little wonder that Jesus turned and rebuked him with such vehemence and force. For through Peter's lips, Satan was taking advantage of an 'opportune time' and attempting to divert Jesus from his path. He was, in a sense, shaking the tightrope. Jesus, of course, does not succumb, but fixes his face towards Jerusalem. Moreover, he uses the incident to teach his disciples about the true meaning of discipleship. In imitation of himself, they are to 'deny themselves, take up their cross and follow me'. Familiar words.

But what does it mean to 'deny yourself'? Does it mean pretending you don't matter, or even that you don't exist? Does it mean trying to suppress your personality and becoming a bland 'non-character', a robot, a drone? Does it mean adopting a harsh asceticism, as an expression of self-hate, in the way encouraged by certain traditions of the early and medieval Church? Jesus teaches his disciples that life's true meaning is found in the service of the Gospel, in being prepared to let go of what the world values, and in choosing to follow him on the way of the cross. In many ways, it was a ridiculous thing to say – like telling people to set out across a tightrope – and carrying a cross at that! Yet it rings true; and it rings true because it is precisely what he himself did in obedience to his heavenly Father.

Today's readings invite us to consider ourselves and the ridiculous nature of our calling – not in a self-indulgent sort of way, but by seeking to discern those aspects of our discipleship where anxiety prevents us from looking forward and causes us to look at our feet. We are invited to ponder the faith of Abraham, about whom St Paul wrote: 'No distrust made him waiver concerning the promise of God,' and to do so in the company of the one who spoke 'quite openly' about the suffering, death and resurrection that awaited him in Jerusalem. May his grace be ours as we do so.

Selflessness is not the absence of the self as subject, but the absence of the self as object of anxious preoccupation. The selfless self can let go.[60]

SECOND SUNDAY OF LENT (ANGLICAN LECTIONARY YEAR C)

If only

Genesis 15:1–12, 17–18
Psalm 27
Philippians 3:17 – 4:1
Luke 13:31–35

Life is full of regrets, or so it sometimes seems: that sense of wishing you had said something when you chose to keep quiet; the guilt that comes with not having done all you had hoped to support that elderly relative, and now she has had a fall. Very often, it's when someone dies that the regrets come into sharpest focus. The 'if onlys' punctuate the conversation, as bereaved friends and relatives speak about the things they didn't manage to do together, the quarrels they didn't manage to put right, that last visit they didn't manage to make, which would have made all the difference had it happened. Such regrets can cause great anguish and are a common feature of the funeral visit, but they more often reflect the guilt felt by the bereaved than their concern for the one who has died.

There is an element of the 'if onlys' in some of our readings today, but it is somewhat different. Here, the anguish is not self-centred, but on behalf of others. St Paul encourages the Philippians to imitate him and not to emulate those who 'live as enemies of the cross of Christ'. As he writes, however, it becomes clear how much he is in anguish because of them: 'I have often told you of them and now I tell you even with tears.' This is not Paul being emotional for its own sake;

rather, he is genuinely distressed because he recognises that 'their end is destruction'. Jesus' lament over Jerusalem carries a similar burden of grief as he mourns the unwillingness of Jerusalem's children to receive his care and protection. Indeed, a little later in Luke's Gospel we read of Jesus, himself, shedding tears over the beloved city and its destiny.

As disciples and ministers of Christ, we stand with confidence and assurance under the loving defence and blessing of our God. Like Abraham and the Psalmist, our trust is in his promised mercy and shelter: he is a shield about us. Yet, does our very confidence prevent us from looking outwards? Do we weep tears over the impending destruction of our neighbours, our friends, members of our family who do not share our faith in Jesus Christ? Are we in anguish because our rebellious and self-satisfied society refuses to acknowledge its need of God?

There is a fine line between complacency and guilt. There may well be more we can do to serve our neighbour and so make Christ known in our own day; there may well be conversations that we know we need to have, to bring truth into our closest relationships and to assuage the anguish we may feel deep down. Perhaps the greatest gift we can offer is in our prayer, as we join our tears with God's in weeping over a world that does not know its need of him. What matters is that when Christ comes again to draw us and all people to himself, we are not left saying, 'If only ...'

When a man becomes a clown he makes a free gift of himself to the audience ... Your Son made the same submission when he was crowned as a mock King and the troops spat wine and water in his face ... My hope is that when he comes again, he will still be human enough to shed a clown's gentle tears over the broken toys that once were women and children.[61]

Notes

1. Cited by Frere Ivan, *Desert and the City*, trans. by Rachel Orbell, St Paul's Publications, 1993, p. 8.
2. Cited by Timothy Ware (ed.), *The Art of Prayer: An Orthodox Anthology*, compiled by Iguen Chariton of Valamo, trans. by E. Kadloubovsky and E. M. Palmer, Faber & Faber, 1966, p. 231.
3. Thomas Merton, *Seeds of contemplation*, Burns & Oates, 1960, p. 108.
4. C. S. Lewis, *Letters to Malcolm: Chiefly on Prayer*, London, 1964, pp. 121–2.
5. Thomas Merton, *Raids on the Unspeakable*, Burns & Oates, 1977, p. 16.
6. Thomas à Kempis, 'How Surrender of Self Brings Freedom of Heart', Chapter 37 in *The Imitation of Christ*, Penguin Books, Harmondsworth, Middlesex, 1952, p. 143.
7. From an address given by Bishop Frank Weston of Zanzibar to the Anglo-Catholic Congress of 1923, in H. Maynard Smith, *Frank, Bishop of Zanzibar: Life of Frank Weston, D.D. 1871–1924*, London, 1926, p. 302.
8. C. F. Andrews, 'The Indentured Coolie', *The Modern Review*, Calcutta, 1915.
9. Donald Coggan, *Meet Paul*, London, 1998, pp. 74–5.
10. Christopher Cocksworth and Rosalind Brown, *Being a Priest Today*, Canterbury Press, 2002, p. 137.
11. Carlo Carretto, *Letters from the Desert*, trans. by Rose Mary Hancock, Darton, Longman & Todd, Maryknoll: Orbis Books, 1972.
12. George Appleton (ed.), from *The Oxford Book of Prayers*, Oxford University Press, 1985, pp. 56–7.
13. H. A. Hodges, in *God and the Universe, A course of sermons preached in the Chapel of Pusey House, Oxford*, London, 1960, pp. 51–3.
14. Vanessa Herrick and Ivan Mann, *Face Value: God in the Place of Encounter*, Darton, Longman & Todd, London, 2002, pp. 80–1.
15. Edward J. Farrell, *Disciples and Other Strangers*, Dimension Books, New Jersey, 1974, p. 27.
16. A. M. Ramsay, *The Glory of God and the Transfiguration of Christ*, Longman, Green & Co., London, 1949, p. 127.

17. Kenneth Bailey, *Finding the Lost: Cultural Keys to Luke 15*, Concordia Publishing House, St Louis, 1992.
18. Jeremy Taylor, 'Worthy Communicant' (1660), in R. Heber and C. Eden (eds), *The Whole Works of Jeremy Taylor*, Vol. II, London, 1850, pp. 628–9.
19. George Herbert, from 'A Priest to the Temple or The Country Parson', in *The Works of George Herbert*, F. E. Hutchinson (ed.), Oxford, 1945 (second, revised edition), p. 233.
20. W. H. Vanstone, from the hymn 'Morning glory, starlit sky', in *Love's Endeavour, Love's Expense*, Darton, Longman & Todd, 1979, pp. 119–20.
21. A monk, *The Hermitage Within*, trans. by Alan Neame, Darton, Longman & Todd, London, 1977, p. 14.
22. Thomas Merton, *No Man is an Island*, Burns & Oates, 1985, p. 209.
23. George Bell, *The Church and Humanity*, London, 1945, pp. 27–8.
24. Carlo Carretto, op. cit.
25. Mary Austell, *The Christian Religion as Profess'd by a Daughter of the Church of England*, London, 1705, pp. 290–1.
26. Thomas à Kempis, op. cit., Chapter 21 'On Contrition of Heart', p. 54.
27. Michel Quoist, *Prayers of Life*, trans. by Anne Marie de Commaile and Agnes Mitchell Forsyth, Gill and Son, Dublin and Melbourne, 1963, p. 2.
28. H. A. Hodges, op. cit.
29. Edwin Sandys, 'The Eleventh Sermon' ('Owe nothing to any man ...'), in *The Sermons of Edwin Sandys*, J. Ayre (ed.), Cambridge (Parker Society), 1842, pp. 204–5.
30. George Herbert, from 'The Collar', *The Works of George Herbert*, op. cit., pp. 144–5.
31. Julian of Norwich, *Revelations of Divine Love*, trans. by Clifton Walters, Penguin, Harmondsworth, 1966.
32. William Shakespeare, *Measure for Measure*, Act II, sc. ii., ll. 117–23, *The Works of William Shakespeare – Comedies*, Paul Alexander (ed.), Collins, London, 1951.
33. St Irenaeus, 'Against all heresies' in Robert Atwell, *Celebrating the Seasons*, Canterbury Press, Norwich, 1999, p. 412.
34. St Augustine, *Confessions. Book 1*, trans. by R. S. Pine-Coffin, Penguin, Harmondsworth, 1961, p. 21.
35. Henri J. M. Nouwen, *The Return of the Prodigal Son: A Story of Homecoming*, Darton, Longman & Todd, London, 1994, p. 102.
36. Dietrich Bonhoeffer, from *Sorrow and Joy*, in *Letters and Papers from Prison*, Eberhard Bethge (ed.), SCM, London, 1953.
37. Julian of Norwich, op. cit., ch. 68.
38. Edward J. Farrell, op. cit., pp. 149–50.

39. Pope Benedict XV. Source unknown.
40. George Bell, op. cit.
41. A Carthusian, *The Wound of Love*, Darton, Longman & Todd, London, 1994.
42. From the Hymnal of Stanbrook Abbey.
43. Words from a hymn. Source unknown.
44. Herbert Kelly SSM, *Catholicity*, London, 1932, pp. 152–3.
45. John Wesley, *Early letters to and about his wife*, Bristol, 11 March 1751. Further source unknown.
46. G. A. Studdert Kennedy, from *The Unutterable Beauty*, Hodder & Stoughton, 1961, pp. 44–8.
47. John A. T. Robinson, in Eric James, *A Life of Bishop John A. T. Robinson: Scholar, Pastor, Prophet*, London, 1987, p. 116.
48. E. Shillito, 'Jesus of the Scars', in J. D. Morrison (ed.), *Masterpieces of Religious Verse*, Harper & Row, New York, 1948.
49. Brother Roger of Taizé. Source unknown.
50. Hebrews 12:1–2.
51. Giles Fletcher (1586–1623), from 'Palm Sunday: Good Friday' in *Poetical Works: Vol. 1 – Giles Fletcher, Phineas Fletcher*, Frederick Samuel Boas (ed.), Cambridge University Press, Cambridge, 1970.
52. Charles de Foucauld, *Letters from the Desert*, Burns & Oates, London, 1977.
53. William Temple, *Readings in St. John's Gospel*, Macmillan & Co. Ltd., London, 1945.
54. Maria Boulding, *Gateway to Hope: An Exploration of Failure*, Collins/Fount, Glasgow, 1985, p. 74.
55. William Temple, *Readings in St. John's Gospel*, op. cit., p. 210.
56. From 'I saw him standing' (from the Welsh of Ann Griffiths) in Rowan Williams, *After Silent Centuries: Poems by Rowan Williams*, The Perpetua Press, Oxford, 1994, p. 46.
57. Alan E. Lewis, *Between Cross and Resurrection: A Theology of Holy Saturday*, Eerdmans, 2001, p. 67.
58. St Augustine, from 'A Sermon for the Octave of Easter', in Robert Atwell, op. cit., p. 236.
59. R. E. C. Browne, from 'Theology of Prayer', in Ian Corbett (ed.), *Love of the World: Meditations*, Worthing, West Sussex, 1986, pp. 96–101.
60. L. Richard, 'Kenotic Christology in a New Perspective', *Église et Théologie* 7, 1976, p. 26.
61. Morris West, *The Clowns of God*, The Toby Press, New Milford, CT, 2003.